Alice Bay Cookbook

Signed!

by Julie Wilkinson Rousseau

Illustrated by Kris Ekstrand Molesworth

J.W. Rousseau

QB

Quartzite Books
Mount Vernon, Washington

For my son, Marcel Joseph

Library of Congress Catalog No. 85-63063
ISBN 0-931849-02-0

Quartzite Books
P.O. Box 1931
Mount Vernon, WA 98273

Manufactured in the United States of America

10 9 8 7 6 5 4 3

CONTENTS

PREFACE

She spreads her green cloak from the rugged Cascade peaks to the sea shores of the San Juans. Beneath her hem, pearly oysters and sweet clams gather close. She trims her skirts with rich farmland, fields of yellow tulips and the greens of broccoli and spinach. Crisp carrots, purple cabbages, and apple blossoms weave a tapestry with golden fields of grain. Salmon thread her rivers as she buttons herself with true blue berries and those of richest red, while Bessie pours the milk and cream.

Here is reason to gather her fresh foods with a pocketful of recipes.

There are rich stories within this Skagit Valley, written on her farms and in her scattered towns. My story begins with my great-grandfather, Jess Hansen Knutzen, Sr., a Danish sea captain who sailed to America with his sweetheart Mette in 1873. Along with thousands of other Scandinavians at the turn of the century, they were attracted to the Northwest by opportunities in farming, logging, and fishing. In 1896, Jess and Mette and their seven sons settled just west of Burlington. Here they farmed 1,000 acres of oats and hay, kept 30 draft horses, 40 sheep, 100 Poland-China hogs, and ran a dairy with 200 head of cattle. By 1900 they had established the Olympic Ridge Creamery and Cheese Factory, and there soon followed a shingle mill and a general store, which sold everything from boots to buggies.

Like many of their fellow Scandinavians, my grandparents and great-grandparents were devout Lutherans. For several years, worshipers gathered in the Knutzen home every Sunday morning for church services. By 1904, the congregation was able to build their own church, still standing today. It is from this church that my most treasured cookbook comes, a gift from my grandmother Anna Knutzen: "Recipes, Burlington Lutheran Church, Burlington, Washington, 1949." This collection of truly special recipes has been lovingly shared by aunts, grandmothers, my mother, and dear women over the years. The red cover is worn with love, and sweet batters smudge the yellowed pages. I was raised on these recipes, and I have included some of them here, for they are the heartbeat of my kitchen.

M. Rousseau
1985

"What is more pleasant than the bond between host and guest?"

Aeschylus

ACKNOWLEDGEMENTS

Here is heartfelt gratitude and thanks from the bottom of my pocketful of recipes, shared by dear friends and family over the years, along with new acquaintances and my favorite cafes. To Terry, for constantly running to the store and being my supper companion; to Marcel, for playing with the egg beaters, and to Gerry for playing pat-a-cake with him. To Georganne and Susan, for baking and being the best big sisters, and to Mother for letting me make a mess in her kitchen with Betty Crocker in the sixties. To Jolene and Dennis, for jotting recipes and dabbling in desserts. To Mel and Wanda, for being next door, and Linda Miller for her grandmother's recipes. To Kris and Claire, for opening the first page, baking blueberries, tasteful advice and editing, drawings and deadlines.

To Gretchen Pickett, Lavonne Newell, Linda Patterson, Anna and Amy Robertson, Dawn Carpenter, Pam Svidran for being ducky, Bernice Merritt, Ann Voorde Porte, Dorothy Anderson, Darlene Hamburg, Grace H. Sakuma, Don and Erin Moe, Julie Pendergrast, Phyllis Moe, Cathy Pfahl, Marie Paule Braule, Anita Guillen, Patricia Hicks, Aunt Marcia and Lela, Roberta, Ann Rasar, Tia Kurtz, Shane and Roz, Rose Wedner, Marsha Polson Belmont, Kari and Ken Vonnegut, Don and Carol Shank, Martin Hahn, Mick and Cheryl August, Tom and Leslie Saunderson, Judy Leber, Karen Leatham, Dave and Dolly Hickox, Carmen Estes, Linda Freed, Ruth Bakke, Bonnie Lehecka, Don Summers, Jim Donovan, Joni Bulfinch, the Skagit County Historical Museum, Beth Hailey, and Pauline.

God bless your food and hands.

SAVORY FARE

I value preparing meals with the freshest and best of foods, sweet creams and butters, crisp valley vegetables, catch of the day seafoods, if just for Marcel's lunch, supper for our family, or dinner with company. I believe that we should eat well. Though it is but a brief part of the day, serve it well. Pause, gain nutrition, some creativity, and bless your food. Here are some of our favorite combinations for special occasions.

A SCANDINAVIAN BAYSIDE BRUNCH

Nutmeg Custard
Buttermilk Aebleskiver
Cream of the Crop
Tea
Coffee

A SAMISH SUPPER

Grilled Oysters
Island Oyster Bake
Oysters Roquefort
Green Garden Salad
Crusty French Bread
Rhubarb Pie
Coffee

A PICNIC BY THE SEA

Sea Pigs with Hot Mustard
Salmon on the Green
Skagit Salad
Sourdough Rolls
Blackberry Brandy
Shortbread Cutouts

A WINTER MEAL TO WARM YOUR COCKLES

Tender Hearts with Crab
Salade Nicoise
Cheesey Bread
Skagit Bouillabaise
Frangos
Coffee

EASTER CELEBRATION FEAST

For our family, the heart and soul of celebrations is reflected in Easter. It is on this day that we invite our families to our home for a festive feast. Being a fourth generation Dane married to a Frenchman in Skagit Valley, America, we color a Greek tradition into our Easter. On Holy Thursday, we dye eggs a deep red to remind us of the blood Christ shed on the cross. The egg is a symbol of the resurrection, containing life motionless, as in the grave, then breaking forth with new life. The cracking of the egg symbolizes the opening of the tomb. On Easter Sunday, after church services, we gather together to crack the brilliant red eggs against each other and proclaim "Christ is risen," and "Indeed, he is risen," and the festive Easter dinner begins.

EASTER DINNER

Dolmathes (Stuffed Grape Leaves)
Seafood in Shells
Retsina, a dry white wine with pure resin added for a
    distinctive taste
Stuffed Tomatoes
Greek Salad
Sausage-Stuffed Leg of Lamb
Ouzo
Honey and Cheese Pie
Greek Coffee
Metaxa, for a final toast of the evening

EASTER EGGS

We use a deep red dye that is available at specialty Greek stores.

24 eggs, washed
5$^1/_2$ cups water
$^3/_4$ cup vinegar
Red dye

In a deep kettle, boil water and vinegar. Add dye and mix well. Add eggs and simmer for 10 minutes. Remove from dye liquid and wipe with oiled cloth to shine.

EATING OUT

There are festive occasions that call for a night on the town, lingering lunches with a friend, or rainy afternoons when a pocketful of change and a warm, cozy cafe are the perfect fare. Several of my favorite cafes and restaurants were kind enough to share some of their special menus, and I've tucked them in for you to try.

THE BLACK SWAN CAFE A SKAGIT NORTHWOODS MEAL

Martin Hahn, owner of The Black Swan storefront cafe in La Conner, is renowned throughout the Northwest for his creative spirit with wild fruits and greens, fresh fish and seafood, and local foods of every description.

Wild Chanterelle Mushroom Timbale
Wild Meadow Green and Edible Flower Salad
Fresh Halibut with Fresh Rhubarb Sauce
Wild Huckleberry Tart

CAFE EUROPA A TOWN TREAT

In downtown Mount Vernon, Ken and Kari Vonnegut of the Cafe Europa serve delightful lunches, generous salads, sandwiches, and daily specials. They feature an irresistible pastry selection, and whenever I'm in town I head straight for one of their tempting European desserts.

Hazelnut Torte
Europa Tart
Cafe Au Lait

CALICO CUPBOARD
A LA CONNER LUNCHEON

At a country-style cafe on La Conner's waterfront, Linda Freed specializes in breakfasts and lunches full of wholesome flavor. The adjoining bakery offers a tantalizing assortment of pastries, desserts, and whole grain breads.

Smoked Salmon Quiche
Honey Wheat Bread
Chocolate Silk Pie

THE MOUNTAIN SONG
A SUMMER SUPPER

Along the North Cascades Highway in Marblemount, The Mountain Song Restaurant serves three hearty meals a day, made with natural and often home-grown ingredients.

Mountain Song Fruit Soup
Oyster Pie or Spinach Quiche
Fresh Fruit Pie

rosemary

THE OYSTER BAR
A SUNSET SPECIAL

The elegant, gourmet Oyster Bar on Chuckanut Drive is owned by Mick and Cheryl August and Tom and Leslie Saunderson. It boasts a beautiful view overlooking Samish Bay, the freshest of oysters, and a variety of imaginative dinners and desserts.

> *Marinated Samish Oysters*
> *Cheese Souffle*
> *Sherry Vinaigrette Salad*
> *Trout with Hazelnuts in Wild Blackberry Sauce*
> *Spinach Timbale*
> *Raspberry Zabaglione*

THE RHODODENDRON CAFE
A NORTHWEST SEAFOOD
DINNER

Located at the Edison crossroads in the middle of the Skagit farmland, the Rhododendron's "Country Fare With A Flair" makes it a popular destination for dinner and weekend brunch. Don and Carol Shank have an adventurous attitude towards fresh local foods, and their blackboard specials are always inviting.

> *Stuffed Mushrooms*
> *Mixed Seafood Salad*
> *King Salmon with Pesto*
> *Fresh Melon Ice*

GOOD MORNING, ALICE

P eter Pan said, "I know a place where dreams are born and time is never told. It's not on any chart, you must find it in your heart."

Though she's not on any chart, Alice Bay tells a colorful story. Long before she had an English name, this sheltered bay on the east end of Samish Island was home to the peaceful Samish Indians. In 1852, "Blanket Bill" Jarman became the first white man to settle on Samish Island, when he and his Clallam wife paddled their canoe from Port Townsend and were welcomed by the Samish chief, S'-yah-whom. Enchanted with the profusion of wild roots and berries, ducks and game, fish and shellfish, and by the beauty of his new surroundings, "Blanket Bill" decided to stay. He named the shallow bay at the mouth of the Samish River after his wife, Alice.

Blanket Bill's arrival was the beginning of an influx of white settlers. By 1875, a logging camp, two stores, a post office, and a small store were established on the island. A steady stream of steamboats pulled into the docks to refuel and drop off freight and passengers for the growing valley settlements. Within one week in 1883, two towns were platted on the island. The first was called Atlanta, and was founded by a Confederate veteran named George Washington Lafayette Allen as "a sanctuary for persecuted Confederates and other sympathizers with the lost cause." Six days later, backed by a group of Union veterans, George Dean platted the town of Samish—separated by one street from Atlanta. A pitched battle of intermittent violence ensued for the next ten years, until the Great Northern Railroad arrived in the valley and replaced the island's importance as a distribution center for the valley. The rival towns and their twin docks soon withered away, and Samish Island settled back into its peaceful character, with small farms and orchards, oyster beds, and scattered homes.

My first home was the Hamilton Hotel, at the base of the North Cascades. Across the street was my father's grocery store, The Cascade Market, where evergreen and Himalayan blackberries sold for fifteen cents a pound. I grew up and moved from the foothills to the bay, to Samish Island. Not a hotel, but with blackberries growing along her driveway, is Alice Bay Bed and Breakfast and my home, a quiet, natural place with a blue heron rookery outside my window, "a sanctuary for people from the city and other guests."

Here I set the table with garden flowers, the aroma of freshly brewed coffee, classical morning music, aebleskiver spiced with cardamom, and warmly welcome our Alice Bay guests to breakfast.

ALICE BAY FRENCH TOAST

Welcome the weekend with this rich and decadent version of an old favorite. Serve with big glasses of freshly squeezed orange juice and a bowl of berries or preserves.

2/3 cup orange juice
1/3 cup Triple Sec or Grand Marnier
1/3 cup milk
1/2 teaspoon vanilla
1/4 teaspoon salt
1/4 cup sugar
6 eggs, beaten
12 thick slices French bread

Garnish: confectioners' sugar

Combine orange juice, Triple Sec, milk, vanilla, salt, and sugar. Add to beaten eggs. Pour over thick slices of French bread and refrigerate overnight.

Heat 2 tablespoons of butter in a heavy skillet and cook slices 5-8 minutes on each side, until golden brown. Dust with confectioners' sugar and serve immediately.

6 portions

Wood stove in the outdoor summer kitchen at Alice Bay.

WALNUT FRENCH TOAST

These are scrumptious pockets of cream cheese and nuts inside egg-drenched French bread drizzled with apricot preserves. For a special brunch, serve with a big bunch of fresh grapes and a chilled bottle of Spumanti.

1 8-ounce package cream cheese, at room temperature
1 teaspoon vanilla
1/2 cup walnuts, chopped
16-ounce loaf French bread
4 eggs
1 cup whipping cream
1/2 teaspoon vanilla
1/2 teaspoon freshly ground nutmeg
12-ounce jar apricot preserves
1/2 cup orange juice

In a small bowl, beat cream cheese and 1 teaspoon of vanilla until fluffy. Stir in nuts.

Cut bread into 10-12 slices about 1 1/2 inches thick. Cut a pocket in each bread slice by slicing from the top halfway to the bottom. Fill pockets with cream cheese mixture.

In a medium bowl, beat eggs, cream, 1/2 teaspoon of vanilla, and nutmeg. Use tongs to dip "sandwiches" into egg mixture. Cook on a lightly greased griddle or skillet over medium heat until brown on both sides. Keep warm in oven.

In a small saucepan, heat preserves and orange juice. Drizzle over top of French toast and serve on warmed plates.

5-6 portions

SWEDISH PANCAKES

These delicate pancakes are an irresistible treat at The Farmhouse Inn between Anacortes and Mount Vernon. They serve their pancakes with Lingonberry Butter made with lingonberries imported from Norway. Canned lingonberry sauce is available at Norwegian specialty shops for the real thing, but the chef also suggests substituting raspberry or blackberry butter for a fresh valley flavor.

> *3 eggs*
> *1 cup half-and-half*
> *1 cup milk*
> *1/2 teaspoon salt*
> *1 tablespoon sugar*
> *1 cup unbleached all-purpose flour*
> *1/2 cup vegetable oil*

In a large bowl, beat eggs until light. Add half-and-half and milk. Sift together salt, sugar, and flour and add to eggs and milk. Beat until smooth. Stir in oil. Let stand for one hour, then beat well and pour a small amount of batter onto a hot skillet — just enough to thinly coat the bottom of the pan. Brown on each side, and keep warm in oven until ready to serve.

LINGONBERRY BUTTER

> *2 cups butter*
> *2 cups margarine*
> *2-3 cups lingonberry sauce or berry preserves*

Mix softened butter and margarine until well blended, and stir in sauce or preserves. Store in a covered container in the refrigerator until ready to use.

GRAND DUTCH BABY

Bring this dutch baby to the table as soon as it comes out of the oven for a grand reception. The classic accompaniments for this dish are confectioners' sugar in a shaker and a bowl of thick lemon wedges. Guests dust the baby with confectioners' sugar and squeeze fresh lemon juice over the top. It is also delicious with a pitcher of warm honey, maple syrup, or homemade berry syrup. When strawberries and raspberries are in season, I serve a big bowl of berries along with the powdered sugar duster. Another popular garnish is orange slices topped with fresh blueberries.

Pan Size	Butter	Eggs	Milk	Flour
2-3 qt.	1/4 cup	3	3/4 cup	3/4 cup
3-4 qt.	1/3 cup	4	1 cup	1 cup
4 1/2-5 qt.	1/2 cup	6	1 1/2 cups	1 1/2 cups

Preheat oven to 425 degrees.

Use the proportion of ingredients to fit your pan size. I use a big cast iron frying pan.

Put butter into pan and place in oven, then quickly mix batter while the butter melts. Put eggs in blender and process at high speed for 1 minute. With motor running, gradually pour in milk, then slowly add flour and continue blending for 30 seconds.

Remove pan from oven and pour the batter into hot melted butter. Return to oven and bake until puffy and golden brown, about 20-25 minutes.

Dust with freshly ground nutmeg and serve at once.

3-6 portions

BLUEBERRY BLINTZES

A bottle of champagne and these crisp golden envelopes make for a luxurious breakfast.

BLINTZES

1 cup unbleached all-purpose flour
2 eggs
1 cup milk
1/4 teaspoon salt
1 teaspoon butter

FILLING

1 1/2 cups ricotta cheese
1 egg, beaten
2 tablespoons sugar
1 teaspoon cinnamon
1/4 teaspoon salt
1 cup fresh blueberries
2 teaspoons butter

Creme fraiche

Place flour, eggs, milk, and salt in blender and whirl until smooth. Refrigerate for 1 hour.

Melt 1 teaspoon of butter in 8-inch crepe pan. Pour in enough batter to thinly coat bottom of pan. Cook both sides until faintly golden, and turn onto a warm plate. Repeat making remaining blintzes, stacking them on the plate as you go.

To prepare the filling, mix together ricotta cheese, egg, sugar, cinnamon, and salt. Gently fold in 3/4 cup of the fresh blueberries. Place a spoonful of filling on each blintz, fold in each end, and gently roll up.

Melt 2 teaspoons of butter in pan and saute blintzes until golden. Serve hot with creme fraiche and sprinkle remaining blueberries over the top.

10 portions

BLINTZ SOUFFLE

A spectacular brunch with sour cream and homemade berry preserves.

FILLING

1 8-ounce package cream cheese, at room temperature
1 pint small curd cottage cheese
2 egg yolks, beaten
1 tablespoon sugar
1 teaspoon vanilla

In a small bowl, beat cream cheese until smooth. Stir in cottage cheese, egg yolks, sugar, and vanilla. Mix well and set aside.

BATTER

$^1/_2$ cup butter, softened
$^1/_3$ cup sugar
6 eggs
1 cup unbleached all-purpose flour
2 teaspoons baking powder
1 $^1/_2$ cups sour cream
$^1/_2$ cup orange juice

Preheat oven to 375 degrees.

In a medium bowl, cream butter and sugar. Add eggs one at a time, beating well after each addition. Measure flour and baking powder and add alternately with sour cream and orange juice to butter mixture.

Pour half of the batter into a greased and floured 9 X 13-inch baking dish. Pour filling over batter and top with remaining batter. Bake for 50 minutes.

8 portions

SIMPLE FRENCH OMELET

3 eggs
1 tablespoon cream
Pinch of salt
1/8 teaspoon freshly ground white pepper
1/8 teaspoon curry, optional

In a medium bowl, beat the eggs until light. Gently whisk in the cream and seasonings.

Heat a medium-sized heavy skillet with rounded bottom and sloping sides. Swirl a tablespoon of butter over surface of pan. When the butter stops foaming, pour egg mixture into the skillet. Cook over medium-high heat until the bottom is set. Using a spatula, move the cooked mixture to the center, allowing the uncooked mixture to flow to the bottom of the skillet.

When the omelet is lightly browned on the bottom, and soft and moist in the center, spoon filling down center. With a heated serving plate in one hand, and the skillet in the other hand, tilt the skillet so that the omelet rolls over onto the plate.

FAVORITE FILLINGS

1. *Sour cream with fresh strawberries and grated orange peel.*
2. *Smoked salmon, creme fraiche, and caviar.*
3. *Poached oysters, fresh tomatoes, and sour cream.*
4. *Mixed fresh vegetables, such as tomatoes, spinach, and sweet onions.*
5. *Lightly sauteed scallops and asparagus.*
6. *Crab meat and sour cream, with curry added to the egg mixture.*
7. *Cheese and chilies.*

1 omelet

OYSTER ROCKEFELLER OMELET

Accompany this rich breakfast with slices of sourdough toast.

SOUR CREAM SAUCE

1 cup sour cream
1 tablespoon Ouzo or Pernod liqueur
1 green onion, minced

OMELET

1 pint fresh shucked oysters
1 bunch spinach, stemmed
8 eggs
1/3 cup cream
1/4 teaspoon hot red pepper sauce
1/2 teaspoon aniseed, crushed
3 tablespoons butter
2/3 cup Parmesan cheese, grated

For sauce, mix sour cream, Ouzo, and green onion in a small bowl and set aside.

In a saucepan, poach oysters in their liquor until edges curl, about 3 minutes. Remove oysters with a slotted spoon and set aside. Add 1/3 cup water to liquor and bring to a boil. Add spinach and blanch for 30 seconds. Remove spinach from liquid, pat dry, and chop.

In a medium bowl, beat eggs until light. Add cream, hot pepper sauce, and aniseed. Mix well.

Melt butter in 10-inch skillet over medium heat. Add eggs and stir quickly, tilting pan to cover surface with egg. When eggs are almost set but still creamy, spread spinach along center of omelet. Lay oysters on top of spinach, and cover with 1/2 cup of sour cream sauce, then sprinkle with cheese. Fold omelet over, enclosing filling in center.

Serve on warm plates, with a small amount of sauce spooned over the top of omelet.

4 portions

HANGTOWN FRY

Start Saturday mornings with a chilled glass of tomato juice and a Hangtown Fry, a spicy oyster and egg dish. Serve with fresh lemon wedges and extra hot sauce.

> *6 eggs*
> *2 tablespoons cream*
> *Dash hot pepper sauce*
> *10 medium oysters, poached*
> *4 slices bacon, chopped*
> *1 small onion, chopped*
> *¹/₄ cup green pepper, chopped*
> *Freshly ground pepper*

Preheat oven to 350 degrees.

In a medium mixing bowl, beat eggs until light and fluffy. Add cream and hot pepper sauce and beat well. Set aside.

In a small saucepan, lightly poach oysters for about 1 minute. Drain and cut each oyster into halves or quarters, depending on size.

In a 10-inch heavy skillet, over medium heat, fry bacon until crisp. Add onions and green pepper and saute until tender-crisp. Add oysters, then the egg mixture. Using a spatula, gently stir the eggs until they just begin to set. Season with pepper. Transfer skillet to oven and bake for about 5 minutes. Watch closely until the eggs puff up slightly, and serve immediately.

2-4 portions

Blaus oyster barge
Samish Island.

CHILE RELLENOS

As valley farmers began widespread cultivation of bulbs, berries, and vegetables, Mexican migrant workers were recruited to harvest the crops. Many of them settled here, and several enterprising families opened popular restaurants throughout the area. Their cuisine has added an exotic flavor to valley cooking. I particularly like this Mexican dinner dish for a lively breakfast.

>*4 whole green chilies, roasted, with seeds and pith removed*
>*1 cup mild Cheddar or Monterey Jack cheese, shredded*
>*2 eggs*
>*2 tablespoons flour*

Prepare salsa and keep warm on stove top.

Stuff chilies with shredded cheese and set aside.

Separate the eggs. In a small bowl, beat egg whites until stiff. In a medium bowl, beat egg yolks until light in color. Add flour to yolks and blend well. Fold in egg whites.

Heat a small amount of oil in a frying pan. Dip stuffed chilies in egg mixture, and fry over medium heat until puffy and golden brown. Serve immediately with bowls of sour cream and salsa.

SALSA

>*1 medium onion, chopped*
>*1 garlic clove, minced*
>*1 medium tomato, diced*
>*1 tablespoon olive oil*
>*8 ounces tomato sauce*
>*2 tablespoons fresh oregano, or 1 teaspoon dried*
>*1 tablespoon chili powder*

In a medium frying pan, lightly saute onion, garlic, and tomato in olive oil. Add tomato sauce, oregano, and chili powder. Simmer gently for 15-20 minutes.

2 to 4 portions

ALICE'S BAKED APPLES

Warm a rainy day's breakfast with these juicy baked apples, hot muffins, and tea.

> 6 *tart apples, washed and cored*
> 3 *tablespoons butter*
> 1/4 *cup brown sugar*
> 1 *teaspoon cinnamon*
> 1/3 *cup dates and/or raisins*
> 1/4 *cup filberts, chopped*
> 1/2 *cup white wine*

Soak Romertopf clay baker in water for 10-15 minutes. If you do not have a Romertopf, butter a shallow baking dish and preheat oven to 300 degrees.

In a mixing bowl, combine 1 tablespoon of butter, sugar, cinnamon, raisins, and filberts. Fill apple cavities with mixture, pressing it in firmly. Dot with remaining 2 tablespoons of butter. Place apples in pot or baking dish and add wine.

Cover and place in the center of a cold oven. Set the oven at 425 degrees and bake for 30 minutes, or until tender. If you do not have a clay baker and are using a baking dish, cook at 300 degrees for 30 minutes, or until tender.

Serve warm with the sweet pan juices.

6 portions

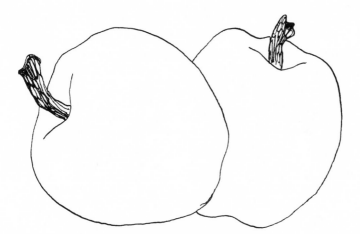

NUTMEG CUSTARD

This nutmeg-sprinkled breakfast custard is nice with fresh strawberries and hot muffins.

1 quart whole milk
6 eggs
¹/₂ cup sugar
1 teaspoon vanilla
Freshly grated nutmeg

Preheat oven to 350 degrees.

Select a pan which is large enough that a 1 ¹/₂-quart custard dish will fit inside it, and water will reach halfway up the sides of the custard dish. Leaving the desired water level in this larger pan, place it in the oven to preheat.

Heat milk in a heavy saucepan until it steams.

In a mixing bowl, beat eggs until light. Add sugar and vanilla and beat until well blended. Gradually stir in warm milk. Pour custard into a shallow 1 ¹/₂-quart baking dish. Generously sprinkle with nutmeg. Set in the preheated water-filled pan and bake, uncovered, for about 45 minutes, until center jiggles slightly when the dish is shaken.

Remove both pans from oven and lift the baking dish from water bath. Let stand for about 10 minutes, then serve custard hot, or chill, covered, as long as overnight.

6-8 portions

BUTTERMILK SCONES

These scones, served with seasonal fruits and freshly ground coffee, are a favorite with our guests at Alice Bay.

> 2 cups unbleached all-purpose flour
> 3 tablespoons sugar
> 2 teaspoons baking powder
> 1/4 teaspoon baking soda
> 1/2 cup cold butter, cut into small pieces
> 1/3 cup raisins
> 1 tablespoon grated orange peel
> 1/2 cup buttermilk
> 1 teaspoon sugar

Preheat oven to 375 degrees.

In a large mixing bowl, combine flour, 3 tablespoons of sugar, baking powder, and soda. Add butter; rub with your fingers to form fine crumbs. Stir in raisins and orange peel. Make a well in the center of the flour mixture and pour in the buttermilk. Stir with a fork until the dough holds together.

Pat the dough into a ball and knead on a lightly floured board for 5 or 6 turns. Divide dough into two parts and shape each half into a smooth ball. Flatten each ball slightly into a 5-inch circle, and cut in half. Place the four semicircles on an ungreased baking sheet, with halves facing each other to form two rounds. Sprinkle with sugar.

Bake for 10 minutes. The scone halves should puff up and touch on their cut edges. With a sharp knife, quickly slash a cross 1/2 inch deep across the tops of the scones. Return to the oven and bake about 20 minutes longer, until golden brown.

The two generous scones should be served warm and broken apart at the table into 4 sections.

4 portions

GRAHAM GEMS

As a child, these muffins were a welcome good morning in Grandma Knutzen's kitchen.

2 cups buttermilk
2 eggs
2/3 cup brown sugar
1 tablespoon shortening
1 teaspoon baking soda
1 teaspoon baking powder
1/2 teaspoon salt
3 cups graham flour

Preheat oven to 400 degrees, and put a greased cast iron muffin pan into oven to preheat while mixing batter.

In a large mixing bowl, mix together the buttermilk, eggs, sugar, and shortening. Add baking soda, baking powder, salt, and flour, and mix thoroughly.

Bake in a preheated muffin pan for about 20 minutes and serve warm.

1 1/2 - 2 dozen muffins

BUTTERMILK AEBLESKIVER

These old-fashioned Scandinavian breakfast puffs are made in a special cast iron pan. They are beautiful as breakfast, and a real treat for a lazy Sunday's supper.

3 eggs
2 tablespoons sugar
2¹/₂ cups buttermilk
3 cups unbleached all-purpose flour
¹/₂ teaspoon salt
1 teaspoon baking powder
1 teaspoon baking soda
¹/₂ teaspoon ground cardamom
¹/₄ cup butter
¹/₄ cup shortening
1 cup prunes, cooked, pitted, chopped and sweetened; or raspberry or strawberry preserves

Confectioners' sugar for dusting

In a large mixing bowl, beat eggs until light. Add sugar and buttermilk and mix well. Sift together flour, salt, baking powder, soda, and cardamom. Gradually add to egg mixture, stirring well after each addition.

Heat aebleskiver pan over medium heat. Melt together butter and shortening. Put 1 tablespoon of butter/shortening mixture in each aebleskiver hole, then fill half full with batter. With a fork, place 1 teaspoon of filling mixture on top of batter. When full of bubbles and browned on the underside, turn each aebleskiver upside down to form a ball, and continue cooking until brown.

Serve warm, rolled in confectioners' sugar, or with preserves.

6 portions

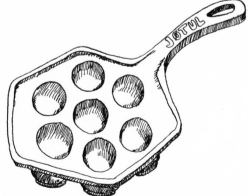

BRAN MUFFINS

Another breakfast at Alice Bay with homemade strawberry preserves. I use a well-seasoned cast iron muffin pan — it gives the finishing light crust these muffins deserve. This batter makes three dozen muffins, so I often use only part of it and store the rest in an air-tight container in the refrigerator. It will keep for up to six weeks.

1 cup boiling water
1 cup Nabisco 100% Bran
2 cups Kelloggs All Bran
1/2 cup shortening
1 1/2 cups sugar
2 eggs, beaten
2 cups buttermilk
2 1/2 cups unbleached all-purpose flour
2 1/2 teaspoons baking soda
1 cup raisins or chopped dates

Preheat oven to 375 degrees.

If you are using a cast iron muffin pan, lightly oil only the bottoms of the muffin cups and preheat in the oven while mixing the batter.

Pour boiling water over brans to soak.

Cream shortening and sugar in a large mixing bowl. Add beaten eggs and buttermilk. Sift together the flour and baking soda and add to egg mixture. Fold in soaked bran and raisins or dates until mixture is moistened throughout.

Fill muffin cups two-thirds full and bake for 15 minutes.

36 muffins

SOUR CREAM BLUEBERRY MUFFINS

These puff up beautifully with flavor.

1/4 cup butter, at room temperature
3/4 cup sugar
2 eggs
1 1/4 cups plus 2 tablespoons sifted all-purpose flour
1/2 teaspoon baking soda
1/4 teaspoon salt
3/4 cup sour cream
1 cup blueberries
1/2 teaspoon vanilla

Preheat oven to 450 degrees, and line muffin tin with paper or foil liners.

In a medium bowl, cream butter and sugar. Add eggs one at a time, beating well. Sift flour, soda, and salt together, and add to butter mixture alternately with sour cream. Gently fold in berries and vanilla.

Bake for 12-15 minutes, until golden brown.

12 muffins

Blueberries

STARLUND'S CARROT MUFFINS

Karen at Starlund's Bakery in Mount Vernon produces an ever-changing assortment of wholesome and inventive pastries and baked goods. These nutty muffins, with their moist texture and hint of pineapple, are especially addictive.

1 cup honey
1 1/4 cups oil
4 eggs
2 1/2 cups whole wheat pastry flour
3/4 teaspoon cinnamon
1/2 teaspoon nutmeg
1/4 teaspoon allspice
1/4 teaspoon salt
3/4 tablespoon baking soda
3 cups grated carrots
10-ounce can crushed unsweetened pineapple
1 cup chopped nuts
1/2 teaspoon Mexican vanilla

Preheat oven to 350 degrees.

In a large mixing bowl, beat the honey and oil together until emulsified. Add the eggs, one at a time, beating well after each addition. Sift together the flour, cinnamon, nutmeg, allspice, salt, and soda. Add to the oil and egg mixture, making sure to blend well, but being careful not to overmix. Add carrots, pineapple, nuts, and vanilla and stir just until mixed well.

Bake in preheated muffin tins for 25 or 30 minutes. This batter keeps well for two weeks in the regrigerator.

36 muffins

DOROTHY'S BLUEBERRY ORANGE BREAD

Gus and Dorothy Anderson tend some 38 acres of blueberries in the valley near Bow. Their fruit stand becomes one of my frequent stops when the season peaks during July and August. Dorothy calls blueberries "the original convenience food" for their ease of preparation and storage. Unwashed berries will stay good and fresh for up to two weeks in the refrigerator if kept dry.

1/2 cup butter
1 1/2 cups sugar
4 eggs
1 1/2 cups orange juice
2 tablespoons grated orange peel
5 cups unbleached all-purpose flour
2 tablespoons baking powder
2 teaspoons salt
1 teaspoon baking soda
1 1/4 cups blueberries, fresh or frozen

Preheat oven to 350 degrees and grease two 9 X 5-inch loaf pans.

In a large bowl, cream together butter and sugar. Beat in the eggs one at a time. Stir in orange juice and peel, then add dry ingredients and mix only until just moistened. Gently fold berries into batter and pour into loaf pans. Bake for 50 minutes, or until a tester inserted in center comes out clean.

2 loaves

TIPS FOR FREEZING BLUEBERRIES

Place dry, unwashed, unsugared berries in freezing containers or plastic bags. Seal and freeze. The berries will freeze individually and pour out like marbles, while washed berries will become mushy upon thawing. Do not freeze berries with sugar, as this makes them tough.

BLUE RIBBON APPLE BREAD

Bonnie Lehecka's ribbon-winning bread from the 8th Annual Samish Island Road Run picnic.

> *¹/₂ cup butter*
> *³/₄ cup brown sugar*
> *2 eggs*
> *¹/₄ cup buttermilk*
> *1 teaspoon vanilla*
> *1 cup chopped apples*
> *³/₄ cup whole wheat flour*
> *³/₄ cup unbleached all-purpose flour*
> *¹/₄ teaspoon salt*
> *³/₄ teaspoon baking soda*
> *³/₄ teaspoon baking powder*
> *¹/₂ cup chopped walnuts*
> *Sugar*
> *Ground cinnamon*

Preheat oven to 350 degrees.

In a large mixing bowl, cream butter and brown sugar. Add eggs, buttermilk, vanilla, and apples; blend well. Sift the flour, salt, soda, and baking powder together and combine with the apple mixture. Fold in the nuts and pour into a greased and floured loaf pan. Sprinkle cinnamon and sugar over top.

Bake for 40-45 minutes.

1 loaf

ORANGE PECAN DATE BREAD

Dense and delicious.

1/4 cup melted butter
1 1/2 cups freshly squeezed orange juice
1/4 cup grated orange peel
1 cup pitted dates, chopped
2 cups sugar
2 eggs, slightly beaten
1 cup pecans or filberts, coarsely chopped
3 1/2 cups sifted unbleached all-purpose flour
1 teaspoon baking soda
2 teaspoons baking powder
1 teaspoon salt

Preheat oven to 350 degrees. Grease and lightly flour a 10 X 5-inch loaf pan.

In a large mixing bowl, blend the butter, orange juice and peel, dates, sugar, eggs, and nuts. Sift together the flour, soda, baking powder, and salt. Fold into batter and mix well.

Pour into a prepared loaf pan. Bake for one hour and cover with foil if the loaf is getting too dark. Bake for another 30 minutes. Cool and coat with orange glaze.

ORANGE GLAZE

1/3 cup sugar
3 tablespoons orange juice concentrate
1/3 cup fresh orange sections, chopped

In a medium saucepan, mix sugar and orange juice concentrate. Stir constantly over low heat for 5 minutes. Remove from heat, add orange sections, and pour over cooled bread.

1 loaf

BESTE'S BANANA BREAD

My mother's recipe, the best I've ever had.

>$^1/_2$ *cup shortening*
>*1 cup sugar*
>*2 eggs*
>*3 very ripe bananas, mashed*
>*3 tablespoons sour milk or buttermilk*
>*1 teaspoon baking soda*
>*2 cups unbleached all-purpose flour*
>$^1/_2$ *cup walnuts, chopped*

Preheat oven to 325 degrees.

Cream shortening and sugar in a mixing bowl. Add eggs, then the bananas and milk. Add soda and flour, and blend well. Stir in nuts. Pour into a greased loaf pan and bake slowly for one hour.

1 loaf

RHUBARB NUT BREAD

An ideal bread for morning coffee.

>$^3/_4$ *cup brown sugar*
>$^3/_4$ *cup white sugar*
>$2^3/_4$ *cups unbleached all-purpose flour*
>*1 teaspoon baking soda*
>$^1/_2$ *teaspoon salt*
>*1 egg*
>*1 teaspoon vanilla*
>*1 cup sour milk*
>$^2/_3$ *cup oil*
>*2 cups diced rhubarb*
>*1 cup chopped walnuts or filberts*

Preheat oven to 350 degrees, and grease and flour two 9 X 5-inch loaf pans.

Mix together brown sugar, white sugar, flour, soda, and salt, and set aside.

In a separate bowl, combine egg, vanilla, and milk. Gradually add dry ingredients and mix well. Add oil, then rhubarb and nuts. Pour into loaf pans and bake for 45-50 minutes, until tester inserted in center comes out clean.

2 loaves

RHUBARB COFFEE CAKE

At 6:30 in the morning I pick the rhubarb fresh from my garden. At 8:00 I serve this coffee cake warm from the oven to our guests at Alice Bay.

> *1/2 cup shortening*
> *1 1/2 cups sugar*
> *1 egg*
> *1 cup buttermilk*
> *2 cups unbleached all-purpose flour*
> *Pinch salt*
> *1 teaspoon baking soda*
> *1 teaspoon vanilla*
> *2 cups finely chopped rhubarb*
>
> *1/2 cup sugar*
> *1 teaspoon cinnamon*

Preheat oven to 350 degrees.

In a large mixing bowl, cream shortening and 1 1/2 cups of sugar. Add egg, and beat until smooth. Add buttermilk, and beat until well mixed. Gradually add the flour, salt, and soda, then the vanilla. Fold in the rhubarb.

Pour batter into an oiled 9 X 13-inch pan. Mix 1/2 cup of sugar with cinnamon and sprinkle over the top. Bake for 35 to 45 minutes.

12 portions

POTICA

I found this surprise bread in my mailbox, a gift from my neighbor Ann Rasar. A rich nut roll made with honey, topped with lots of icing and chopped nuts, and no postage, Potica is a traditional Slovenian recipe. In the 1890's and 1900's, a wave of Slovenians and their neighboring Croatians emigrated here from the Northern Adriatic coast. Accustomed to a fishing culture, many of them settled around Anacortes, where they continued to make their living from the sea.

2 cups milk
3/4 cup sugar
2 packages active dry yeast
2/3 cup warm water
2 teaspoons salt
7 heaping cups unbleached all-purpose flour
4 eggs
1/2 cup butter, melted

In a large saucepan, scald milk over medium heat. Add sugar and stir until dissolved. Set aside and let cool.

In a small bowl, stir two packages of yeast into warm water. In a large bowl, combine cooled milk/sugar mixture with raised yeast. Add salt and 2 cups of flour. Beat with an electric mixer for 2 minutes. Add eggs and melted butter and beat for 1 minute more. Gradually add the rest of the flour.

Knead for 15 minutes. Cover dough and let rise for 1 hour, until doubled in size. Make the nut filling while the dough rests.

NUT FILLING

2 cups milk
2 pounds pecans, chopped
6 eggs
2 cups honey
1 cup sugar
2 teaspoons vanilla
2 teaspoons cinnamon
16-ounce carton cottage cheese

In a medium saucepan, scald milk. Add nuts, and let the mixture come to a boil, stirring constantly. Add eggs one at a time, beating well after each addition. Then add honey, sugar, vanilla, and cinnamon. Mix well, and cook for 5 minutes over low heat. Remove from heat, stir in cottage cheese, and cool.

To assemble, cover a large table or working surface with a floured pastry cloth. Place ¼ of the dough in center of cloth and roll out very thin into a rectangular shape. Spread 2 cups of the filling all the way to the edges of the dough. Roll the dough carefully from one edge to form a long roll. Place on a greased baking sheet in the shape of an S. Repeat with rest of dough. Cover with a clean cloth and let rise until doubled. Gently prick dough before baking.

Preheat oven to 300 degrees, and bake for 1 hour. Cool, and spread Powdered Sugar Icing over the top.

POWDERED SUGAR ICING

¼ cup milk
2 cups sifted confectioners' sugar
1 teaspoon vanilla
Dash of salt

Combine milk and sugar and blend until mixture reaches spreading consistency. Stir in vanilla and salt.

Croatian purse seiners; San Juan Island 1901

VINABROD

This flaky pastry is traditionally shaped into three spiral loaves. It would be equally nice as individual crescents.

> *3 packages active dry yeast*
> *1 1/2 cups lukewarm milk*
> *1 egg and 1/2 of another egg (reserve other 1/2)*
> *1 tablespoon sugar*
> *1 teaspoon salt*
> *3-4 cups unbleached all-purpose flour*
> *1 cup butter, cut into small pieces*

FILLING

> *1/2 cup butter, at room temperature*
> *1 1/2 cups sugar*
> *1 1/2 teaspoon almond extract*
> *3/4 cup chopped walnuts*

Dissolve yeast in lukewarm milk, and allow to proof for a few minutes. Add eggs, sugar, salt, and flour to the yeast mixture and stir well. Transfer dough to a floured board and knead lightly.

Roll dough into a rectangular shape about 1/4 inch thick. Distribute one third of the butter pieces onto half of the rectangular dough and fold in half over butter. Roll dough into a rectangle again, and place another third of the butter onto half of the dough. Fold, roll out, and repeat once more. Roll dough until it is 1/4 inch thick. Cut into 3 strips about 5 inches wide.

Blend filling ingredients in bowl or food processor. Spread filling down the center of each strip of dough. Fold dough over filling or roll gently into long loaves. Seal ends. Brush loaves with beaten egg yolk and cut a few diagonal slashes in the tops of the loaves. Let rise for 1 hour.

Preheat oven to 350 degrees, and bake for 25-30 minutes.

3 loaves

GREAT
Beginnings

Stuffed Mushrooms.

WATERCHESTNUT CRAB DIP

The waterchestnuts and crab blend interestingly for a refreshing appetizer. I like to serve this in an oversized sea shell. Besides crackers, celery sticks and green pepper strips dip with great zest.

1 cup mayonnaise
1 teaspoon soy sauce
3 green onions, chopped
8-ounce can waterchestnuts
2 cups crab meat

Mix the mayonnaise, soy sauce, and chopped green onions together. Shred the waterchestnuts and add with crabmeat.

2 cups

TENDER HEARTS

Pick and choose from these versatile dips. Serve with fresh vegetable sticks and flowerets, tortilla chips, or breadsticks.

WITH CHILIES

14-ounce can unmarinated artichoke hearts
4-ounce can mild green chilies, rinsed and chopped
1 cup mayonnaise
1 cup Parmesan cheese, grated

Mix all ingredients together; heat at about 375 degrees until bubbly.

WITH CRAB

14-ounce can unmarinated artichoke hearts
6-7 ounces fresh or canned crab
1 1/2 cups mayonnaise
1 cup Parmesan cheese, grated

Same method as above.

WITH WHOLE BABY CLAMS

14-ounce can unmarinated artichoke hearts
1 large can whole baby clams
1 1/4 cups mayonnaise
1 cup Parmesan cheese, grated

Drain clams well. Same method as above.

MARINATED OYSTERS

This wonderful appetizer is a popular beginning for dinner at the Oyster Bar, along with one of their superb Northwest wines.

36 Samish Bay yearling oysters
1 1/2 cups white wine
1/2 cup red wine vinegar
1/2 cup olive oil
2/3 cup plus 2 tablespoons lemon juice
1/2 teaspoon salt
1/2 teaspoon pepper
1/2 teaspoon thyme
1/2 teaspoon dried chervil
2 tablespoons finely minced parsley
3/4 ounce minced garlic
1/2 cup Walla Walla sweet onions, minced
2 tablespoons dried chives

Mix marinade ingredients well, add oysters and let stand for 15 minutes. After 15 minutes, heat to a boil and then remove oysters immediately. Pour into a different pan and refrigerate until well chilled.

6 portions

ANGELS ON HORSEBACK BY THE WATER

A crisp appetizer made of oysters and waterchestnuts wrapped in bacon. Wash these down with plenty of cold beer.

24 small oysters, shucked
1 5-ounce can whole waterchestnuts
1 pound bacon, cut into half lengths

In a saucepan, lightly poach oysters in their own liquor. Drain.
In a frying pan, cook bacon just until limp.
Preheat oven to 425 degrees.
Wrap each oyster and waterchestnut separately with a bacon slice. Secure with toothpicks. Broil on rack in oven or grill over charcoal for about 5-10 minutes, until bacon is lightly crisp. Watch carefully and turn occasionally. Drain on paper towels if necessary. Serve hot.

8 portions

ABALONE BEACHBALLS

We dive for abalone on our sailing trips to the San Juans. Even if you hunt yours at the market, this is a fun way to serve them.

4-6 whole abalone, cut into steaks and pounded
¹/₄ cup soy sauce
¹/₄ cup sake or tequila
8-ounce can water chestnuts, whole or halved
Several strips of bacon
Toothpicks

In a medium-sized bowl, mix soy sauce and sake. Slice abalone steaks into ¹/₂-inch wide strips, and marinate in soy sauce mixture for 2 hours. Drain.

Wrap each strip of abalone around a waterchestnut. Secure with a toothpick through abalone and nut. Place on a cookie sheet. Lay strips of bacon over the abalone bundles.

Broil until bacon is lightly crisp. Remove bacon and discard, otherwise the flavor will smother the abalone. Place the abalone on a heated serving dish and serve hot to your guests.

CEVICHE

A fresh taste of the sea.

1 cup bay scallops
Juice of 1 large lime
1 green onion, sliced
1 small white onion, minced
¹/₃ cup fresh parsley, minced
¹/₃ cup tomato, chopped, with seeds removed

Combine these ingredients in a small glass bowl. Cover and refrigerate. Chill for at least four hours before serving.

4 portions

SEA PIGS

The clams come from the sea, the pork from the pig, hence sea pigs. An unusual combination, but one that always gets rave reviews at Alice Bay. I serve these with the same Spicy Mustard that I use for Duck Strips; use this or your own favorite hot mustard.

> *1 pint clams, ground*
> *1 pound pork sausage*
> *1 small onion, grated*
> *2 cloves garlic, pressed*
> *1 cup plain bread crumbs*
> *1 egg, beaten*
> *1 teaspoon fresh marjoram*
> *Freshly ground pepper*
> *Seasoned bread crumbs*
> *Oil*

Combine clams, sausage, onion, garlic, plain bread crumbs, egg, marjoram, and pepper. Mix well with hands. Roll into small balls, using about 1 tablespoon of the mixture for each ball. Roll in seasoned bread-crumbs.

Up to this point, recipe may be prepared early in the day and then refrigerated, ready to pan fry and serve hot when your guests arrive.

In a heavy skillet, heat a small amount of oil on about medium to medium-low heat. Panfry the meatballs until golden and crispy on the outside, about 10 minutes. Drain any excess oil off meatballs on paper towels. Then transfer to a heated serving platter and serve with hot mustard. Toothpicks are your utensils.

60 small meatballs

STUFFED MUSHROOMS

An unbeatable beginning for supper with a Sauvignon Blanc, compliments of the Rhododendron Cafe.

> *1/2 cup onions, diced*
> *1/2 cup walnuts, chopped*
> *2 apples, peeled, cored, and diced*
> *1/2 teaspoon salt*
> *1/2 teaspoon pepper*
> *1 teaspoon dill*
> *1 cup baby shrimp*
> *1/4 cup butter*
> *4 dozen large mushrooms*
> *1/4 cup bread crumbs*
> *Olive oil*

Preheat oven to 425 degrees.

Put onions, walnuts, apples, salt, pepper, dill, and shrimp in food processor or blender and pulse for 3-5 seconds. Do not puree — whiz quickly so as to lightly mince.

Saute entire mixture in butter for 4-5 minutes over medium heat, stirring constantly.

Pull stems from large mushrooms and place caps upside down on baking tray. Mound with stuffing mixture, sprinkle with bread crumbs, and drizzle with olive oil.

Bake for 7-9 minutes.

48 appetizers

MUSHROOMS MILANO

Try these mushrooms stuffed with fresh spinach and cheese for a rich intro.

12 large or 36 medium fresh mushrooms
1 tablespoon melted butter
1 tablespoon peanut oil
1 bunch fresh spinach
1 cup ricotta cheese
1 clove garlic, minced
Pinch freshly ground pepper
1/3 cup grated Parmesan or sharp Gruyere cheese

Preheat oven to 400 degrees.

Wash and dry mushrooms. Remove stems and mince finely. Mix melted butter and oil and brush caps thoroughly. Arrange caps upside down on baking sheet. Wash the spinach and drain well. Remove stems and chop leaves finely. Combine chopped spinach with ricotta cheese, garlic, and pepper.

Spoon mixture into mushroom caps and top with grated Parmesan cheese. Bake in a hot oven for 10 minutes, until hot throughout.

36 appetizers, about 12 portions

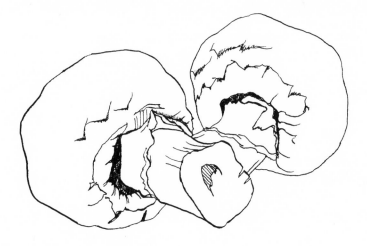

ALBONDIQUITAS

The Latin Connection or Some Like It Hot or Migrants Meet the Meatballs: Jim Donovan's award-winning meatball at the Samish Island Road Run and Potluck in our backyard. The French eat these with their fingers, Swedes with toothpicks.

>2 jalapeno peppers
>1 1/2 pounds ground beef
>1 egg
>3 green onions, including stalks, chopped
>1 clove garlic, chopped
>2/3 cup dry bread crumbs
>1/3 cup milk
>1/2 cup Montery Jack or Cheddar cheese, shredded
>1/3 teaspoon pepper or 12 twists on the mill

Preheat oven to 400 degrees.

Remove stems, seeds, and membranes from chilies—you may want to wear rubber gloves for this operation. Chop chilies and mix with rest of ingredients. Refrigerate overnight if you want it very spicy—otherwise, proceed—it's spicy already.

Shape mixture into 1-inch balls, and place on 13 X 9-inch cookie sheet or pan. Cook uncovered until brown, about 15-20 minutes. Transfer to serving dish and slather with salsa.

SALSA

>15-ounce can tomato sauce
>1 tomato, chopped
>2 cloves garlic, minced
>2 tablespoons fresh parsley, snipped
>1 tablespoon vinegar
>1/4 teaspoon cumin

Combine ingredients in saucepan, heat, and eat.

50-60 meatballs

DUCK STRIPS WITH HOT MUSTARD

This duck is sweet and moist, with the pungent mustard a tasty prelude to a harvest dinner, or alone with plenty of chilled lager beer and hunting stories.

6 duck breasts
Krustez Bake & Fry Mix
Freshly ground pepper
Peanut oil

Skin duck breasts and cut into 1/4-inch strips. Dredge duck strips in dry mix with pepper.

Heat peanut oil in wok or heavy frying pan. Fry duck strips in batches until brown and lightly crisp—about 2 minutes per batch. Drain on paper towels, and keep warm on serving platter in oven.

Serve with Spicy Mustard.

4-6 portions

SPICY MUSTARD

1 cup dry mustard
6 tablespoons beer
6 tablespoons molasses
6 tablespoons apple cider vinegar
1/2 teaspoon ground allspice
1/2 teaspoon ground cinnamon
1/2 teaspoon salt
1/2 teaspoon freshly ground pepper
1/4 teaspoon ground cloves

Whisk mustard and beer together in stainless steel bowl until well blended. Let stand for about 15 minutes. Add molasses, vinegar, and spices and blend thoroughly.

Transfer to jar and cap tightly. Store in a cool, dark place.

1 cup

LAYERED APPETIZER TORTE

Layers of sausage, Cheddar cheese, and green onion combine for a spicy pate.

> *3 8-ounce packages cream cheese, at room temperature*
> *6 tablespoons butter*
> *1 cup minced sausage, cooked*
> *1 tablespoon minced onion*
> *Dash hot pepper sauce*
> *2 cups grated medium Cheddar cheese, at room temperature*
> *5 green onion tops*

Layer 1: Combine and beat until smooth: 8 ounces of softened cream cheese and 2 tablespoons of butter. Add the cooled sausage, 1 tablespoon of minced white onion, and a dash of hot pepper sauce. Spread in the bottom of an 8-inch springform pan, smoothing carefully. Wipe edges clean. Chill.

Layer 2: Combine and beat until smooth: 8 ounces of softened cream cheese and 2 tablespoons of butter. Add 2 cups of grated Cheddar and 2-3 tablespoons of milk to make it about the same consistency as the first layer. Spread over top of meat layer. Smooth out and clean edges as needed. Chill.

Layer 3: Combine and beat until smooth: 8 ounces of softened cream cheese and 2 tablespoons of butter. Wash and shake dry 5 green onion tops. Puree green onion tops and add to cheese mixture. Beat until completely blended. Spread over cheese layer as before. Chill well.

Unmold by running a knife around the edges of the pan and removing ring. Garnish with parsley and serve with crackers and cocktail loaves.

WILD CHANTERELLE MUSHROOM TIMBALE BLACK SWAN

The rainy foothills of the North Cascades shelter the delicate chanterelle. Martin Hahn of the Black Swan is an artist at using them.

> *2 pounds chanterelle mushrooms*
> *2 tablespoons sweet butter*
> *3 cups warm milk*
> *8 beaten eggs*
> *1¹/₂ teaspoons salt*
> *1 teaspoon paprika*
> *¹/₄ teaspoon nutmeg*
> *1 tablespoon chopped fresh tarragon or 1 teaspoon dried*
> *1 tablespoon chopped fresh parsley*
> *Juice of 1 lemon*
> *1 tablespoon Dijon mustard*

Preheat oven to 375 degrees.

Saute chanterelles in butter. Remove from heat and set aside to cool.

Custard Base: Warm milk and add to beaten eggs. Add salt, paprika, nutmeg, tarragon, parsley, lemon juice, and mustard. Mix well, and fold custard base into sauteed mushrooms.

Butter timbale molds (or other type of mold) and pour in mushroom custard mixture. Bake until firm, about 20 to 25 minutes. Serve with Tarragon Vinegar Bernaise Sauce.

TARRAGON VINEGAR BERNAISE SAUCE

> *8 egg yolks*
> *2 tablespoons tarragon vinegar*
> *1 tablespoon fresh tarragon*
> *1 teaspoon minced shallots*
> *2 cups butter, clarified and melted*

Whirl egg yolks in food processor or blender.

In a small saucepan, combine the vinegar, tarragon, and shallots, and reduce by half. Add vinegar mixture to egg yolks and whirl for 30 seconds. Add melted clarified butter in slow stream until well blended.

TO CLARIFY BUTTER

Melt butter over low heat. When completely melted, remove from burner and let cool until milk sediments settle to the bottom of the pan. Skim the clear butter fat off the top and strain into a clean container.

SMOKED SALMON AND CAPER WHIP

Equally welcome at a fancy luncheon or plain picnic.

1 8-ounce package cream cheese, at room temperature
1/4 cup fresh parsley leaves
2 tablespoons fresh lemon juice
1 tablespoon heavy cream
1 teaspoon capers, rinsed and drained
4 ounces smoked salmon

Cocktail rye bread
2 medium tomatoes, cored and sliced
2 medium onions, thinly sliced
Capers, rinsed and drained

Combine cream cheese, parsley, lemon juice, cream, and 1 teaspoon of capers with 3 ounces of the smoked salmon and mix until smooth. Add remaining salmon and mix briefly until just incorporated, retaining texture of salmon as much as possible.

Spread salmon whip on sliced rounds of bread. Top with thinly sliced onion, sliced tomato, and a few capers.

2 dozen appetizers

SALMON PATE

An elegant first course.

> $^1/_2$ *cup shrimp or chicken stock*
> *1 tablespoon unflavored gelatin*
> *8 ounces canned red salmon*
> $^1/_4$ *cup mayonnaise*
> $^1/_2$ *cup whipping cream*
> *4 tablespoons fresh parsley, minced*
> *2 teaspoons lemon juice*
> *2 green onions, roughly chopped*
> *Dash of white pepper*

Heat stock and place in food processor or blender with gelatin. Blend for 2 minutes. Add undrained salmon and remaining ingredients. Blend until smooth, and pour into a lightly greased small mold. Refrigerate until set.

When ready to serve, pour a small amount of green horseradish sauce on a flat round serving dish. Unmold pate onto center of dish. Serve additional sauce in a small bowl.

GREEN HORSERADISH SAUCE

> *1 egg*
> *1 egg yolk*
> *1 teaspoon prepared mustard*
> $^1/_2$ *cup chopped fresh parsley*
> *1 tablespoon white vinegar*
> *1 cup oil*
> *1 tablespoon finely grated horseradish*
> *Salt*
> *Freshly ground pepper*

In blender, put 1 whole egg, egg yolk, mustard, parsley, and vinegar. Blend for 1 minute. Gradually add oil until $^1/_2$ cup of oil has been added and mixture has begun to thicken. Slowly add remaining oil. Add horseradish and seasonings. Blend well. Chill before serving.

4-6 small portions

CHICKEN LIVER PATE

Pates serve so well for elaborate occasions, country buffets, or simply when one wants to open the refrigerator and pull out a midnight snack to be spread on a thin slice of dense wheat bread. This is a good one.

3 teaspoons butter
3 green onions, chopped
1 pound chicken livers
1/2 cup red wine
1/4 teaspoon salt
1/2 teaspoon fresh thyme or 1/8 teaspoon dried
1/8 teaspoon freshly ground pepper
4 tablespoons fresh parsley, chopped
1 cup butter, cut into pieces, at room temperature

In a frying pan, saute onions in 3 teaspoons of butter until limp. Add chicken livers and cook, turning, for 6 minutes. Add wine, salt, thyme, and pepper. Simmer for 3 minutes. Add parsley and transfer into food processor or blender. Process until smooth. With motor running, gradually add butter. Continue to process until well blended. Cover and chill for up to 4 days.

CHEESE SOUFFLE

An Oyster Bar favorite of ours.

1/2 cup butter
1/2 cup all-purpose flour
1 1/2 teaspoons salt
1/2 teaspoon paprika
3 drops Tabasco
2 1/2 cups milk
1 cup grated Cheddar cheese
10 egg whites
1/4 teaspoon cream of tartar
8 egg yolks

Preheat oven to 425 degrees.

Melt butter in top of double boiler. When melted, add flour, salt, paprika, and Tabasco. Whisk until smooth.

Meanwhile, put milk on to boil. When milk begins to rise up in the pan, add it to the butter and flour mixture. Whisk until thick and smooth. Add cheese. Remove from boiler and let rest for 1 minute.

Start whipping the egg whites slowly. When a froth forms, add the cream of tartar. Meanwhile, add the egg yolks one at a time to the flour-butter mixture and whisk rapidly. Set aside to cool. When the whites hold a gentle peak, fold a spatula-full into the cheese base and work it in. Then fold in the rest of the whites.

Portion into buttered and floured individual souffle cups and bake for 20 minutes.

6 portions

ROASTED FILBERTS

On Sunday afternoons we enjoy the sweet flavor of roasted filberts with a chilled bottle of champagne and lots of conversation.

Spread shelled filberts in a shallow pan and toast in a 275 degree oven for 20 minutes, or until the skins crack. Use with the tender skin, or remove the skin by rubbing nuts between your hands while still warm.

We are lucky to live in a part of the country where filberts thrive. Buy fresh nuts in the fall, or get permission to gather a supply from one of the old orchards around the valley. These nuts freeze beautifully.

SKAGIT
SOUPS

CLAM VELVET

This rich and creamy chowder makes a delightful supper with a big fresh spinach salad and crusty bread.

> 3 cups cooked, chopped clams
> 4 cups clam nectar
> 1 quart half-and-half
> 1 1/2 pounds Swiss cheese, grated
> 1/2 cup fresh chives, chopped
> 1 cup red bell pepper, finely diced
> 1 tablespoon salt
> 1 tablespoon white pepper
> 1 1/2 tablespoons fresh thyme or 1/2 tablespoon dried
> 2-3 large garlic cloves, pressed
> 2 cups dry white wine
> 2 cups butter
> 1 1/2 cups all-purpose flour

In a 6-quart double boiler, place clams, clam nectar, half-and-half, and cheese. Place over low heat until the liquid becomes quite warm, then add chives, bell pepper, salt, pepper, thyme, and garlic.

In a saucepan over high heat, reduce the wine by half its volume and add to clam mixture.

In another saucepan over medium heat, melt the butter and slowly add flour to make a roux. Cook flour in butter, stirring constantly, until it is well thickened but not browned.

When ingredients in double boiler are hot enough to steam, add roux, slowly blending in with a wire whip. Cook for 45 minutes over low heat. Do not allow to boil. If soup does not thicken properly, add a little more roux. If soup is too thick, thin with half-and-half.

1 gallon

SKAGIT BOUILLABAISSE

A fantastic fish stew using local ingredients.

4 pounds whitefish fillets, cut into 1 or 2-inch pieces
2 pounds bay scallops
24 steamer clams, steamed and drained. Reserve the nectar.
24 blue mussels, steamed and drained
2 pounds shrimp, shelled and deveined
Olive oil
3 medium onions, chopped
4 stalks celery, chopped
1 green pepper, diced
2 carrots, sliced
3 cloves garlic, minced
2 cups dry white wine
2 cups clam nectar, or fish stock
2 large cans whole tomatoes, cut up
1 quart tomato juice or Snappy Tom
Dash of hot pepper sauce
1 teaspoon saffron
¹/₂ teaspoon fennel seed, crushed
2 bay leaves
¹/₄ cup minced fresh parsley
Freshly ground pepper

Heat olive oil in a large skillet or soup pot. Add onions, celery, green pepper, carrots, and garlic. Saute until transparent, about 3 minutes.

Add wine, clam nectar, tomatoes and their juice, tomato juice, hot pepper sauce, saffron, fennel seed, and bay leaves. Simmer for 5 minutes.

Add fish pieces and scallops. Simmer for 5-7 minutes. Stir in clams, mussels, shrimp and parsley. Simmer for 3-5 more minutes, until shrimp are tender and clams and mussels are heated through.

Spoon into large soup bowls and serve piping hot.

16 portions

SCANDINAVIAN SEAFOOD STEW

For a party dinner, accompany this full-flavored stew with Swedish Limpa bread and a dry Chablis.

1 pound tiny onions, peeled
1 cup chopped cabbage
2 medium carrots, finely chopped
1 1/2 pounds new potatoes, scrubbed and cut into small cubes
3 tablespoons butter
1 tablespoon fresh thyme
1 tablespoon minced fresh dill
3/4 teaspoon minced fresh savory
1/8 teaspoon ground cardamom
7 cups fish stock
1 pint canned clams, drained, or 1 1/2 pounds fresh clams
1 pound medium shrimp, shelled and deveined
2 pounds cod fillet, cut into bite-sized pieces
1/2 cup whipping cream or creme fraiche
1/4 teaspoon salt
1/4 teaspoon freshly ground pepper

Garnish: 1/2 cup minced green onion tops

Combine onions, cabbage, carrot, potatoes, butter, herbs, and cardamom in a heavy non-aluminum 6-quart pot. Cover and cook over low heat until the cabbage and carrots are tender, about 10 minutes. Add the fish stock and simmer until onions and potatoes are crisp-tender, about 30 minutes.

Add clams, shrimp, and cod. Cook until barely firm, about 2-3 minutes longer. Stir in cream and season to taste with salt and pepper. Do not allow the fish to overcook.

Serve immediately, sprinkling onion tops over each bowl.

8 portions

SPICED FISH STOCK

This is the stock I always use for Seafood Stew and fish sauces. I collect trimmings from whitefish and salmon and store them in the freezer until I have accumulated enough to start a stock pot.

5-6 pounds fish trimmings (bones, heads, tails)
2 large onions, quartered
2 large carrots, sliced
26 whole white peppercorns
4 unpeeled garlic cloves
4 whole allspice berries
3 whole cardamom pods
2 parsley sprigs
4 whole cloves
1 tablespoon fresh thyme
Salt
1 bottle dry white wine
2 quarts cold water

Place fish trimmings in a large, heavy, non-aluminum pan. Add the onion, carrot, peppercorns, garlic, allspice, cardamom, parsley, cloves, thyme, and salt. Cover and cook over medium-low heat until fish has released its juices, about 15 minutes, watching carefully to avoid burning. Add wine and water and slowly bring to a simmer. Partially cover and simmer gently for 90 minutes. Strain through a sieve or cheesecloth.

Stock can be made 1 or 2 days ahead and refrigerated, or frozen for up to 3 months.

2 quarts

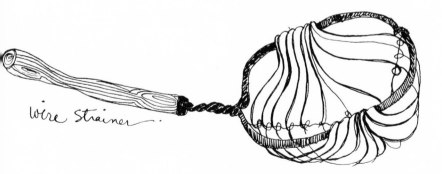

Wire Strainer

OYSTER STEW NIPPON

A bowl of this exquisite soup and steamed rice make a simple evening meal. Instead of the classic chicken soup when you have a winter cold, nurse yourself with this nourishing stew.

> *6 cups chicken broth*
> *2 tablespoons soy sauce*
> *1 teaspoon grated ginger root*
> *1 pint shucked oysters*
> *2 cups chopped Chinese cabbage*
> *8 ounces sliced mushrooms*
> *1/2 cup bean sprouts*
> *6 ounces Chinese pea pods*
> *4 green onions, cut into 1-inch pieces with tops*

In a large saucepan, heat chicken broth, soy sauce, and ginger root to a full boil. Add oysters with their liquid, then cabbage, mushrooms, bean sprouts, and pea pods. Heat to boiling and reduce heat. Cover and simmer until cabbage is tender-crisp, about 2 minutes. Add the green onions.

Ladle soup into bowls and serve immediately.

4 portions

CHILLED STRAWBERRY SOUP

This rosy Scandinavian soup makes a stunning first course with grilled salmon.

> *2 pints fresh strawberries, washed and hulled*
> *1 cup freshly squeezed orange juice*
> *1 1/4 teaspoons instant tapioca*
> *1/8 teaspoon ground allspice*
> *1/8 teaspoon cinnamon*
> *1/2 cup sugar*
> *1 teaspoon grated lemon peel*
> *1 tablespoon freshly squeezed lemon juice*
> *1 cup buttermilk*
>
> *Garnish: 1 lemon, thinly sliced*

Set aside 6 strawberries. Puree remaining berries in a food processor or blender, and strain into a saucepan. Add the orange juice.

In a small bowl, mix tapioca with 1/4 cup of the pureed strawberry mixture. Return to saucepan along with allspice and cinnamon. Heat, stirring constantly, until mixture comes to a boil. Cook until thickened, and remove from heat.

Pour soup into a large bowl. Add sugar, lemon peel and juice, and buttermilk. Blend well. Slice the reserved strawberries and fold into soup. Cover and chill for at least 8 hours.

Serve the chilled soup with a lemon slice floating in each bowl.

4 portions

MOUNTAIN SONG FRUIT SOUP

A scenic drive up the Skagit River will lead you to a naturally wonderful restaurant, The Mountain Song, and a bowl of this vibrant chilled soup.

1/2 pound fresh raspberries, strawberries, blueberries, or blackberries
1 quart water
1 tablespoon tapioca
1/4 cup cold water
1 tablespoon lemon juice
2 tablespoons sugar
1/4 cup white wine

Garnish: whipped cream

Reserve a few whole ripe berries. Cook the rest of the berries in water until soft. Drain and reserve juice.

Puree the cooked fruit briefly in a blender or food processor, adding a small amount of juice as needed.

Dissolve tapioca in cold water and add to berry liquid. Mix together and cook over medium heat until tapioca is transparent. Add lemon juice and sugar to taste. Allow to cool. Stir in white wine.

Garnish each bowl with a few ripe berries and a spoonful of whipped cream.

8 portions

COLD CUCUMBER-MINT SOUP

As cool as a cucumber on hot summer evenings.

3 medium cucumbers
3 tablespoons butter
1 medium onion, chopped fine
1 clove garlic, minced
3 tablespoons flour
3 cups chicken stock
2 tablespoons finely chopped fresh mint
1 cup half-and-half
Salt
Freshly ground white pepper

Garnish:
Sliced cucumber
Sprigs of fresh mint

Peel and slice cucumbers very thin. Melt butter in a large skillet over medium heat. Add onion and garlic and saute until limp. Do not brown. Add sliced cucumber and cook slowly until soft, and remove from heat.

Stir in flour, then chicken stock and mix well. Place over medium-high heat and bring to a boil. Reduce heat and simmer for 5 minutes. Puree soup in a blender or food processor. Pour into a large mixing bowl and stir in mint. Cover and chill well.

Just before serving, stir in half-and-half and blend well. Season to taste with salt and pepper. Garnish each bowl with sliced cucumber and a sprig of fresh mint.

6 portions

GAZPACHO

Invite some friends over on a Thursday evening and serve this cold garden soup to kick off a full Italian meal, then savor it alone for Saturday lunch.

2 cups chopped peeled tomatoes
1 cup chopped green pepper
1 cup chopped celery
1 cup chopped cucumber
1/2 cup chopped onion
1/8 cup fresh chopped parsley or 4 teaspoons dried
1 teaspoon chili pepper
1 teaspoon cayenne pepper
4 teaspoons fresh chives or 2 teaspoons dried
2 garlic cloves, pressed
5 tablespoons wine vinegar
4 tablespoons olive oil
2 tablespoons salt
1/2 teaspoon ground pepper
1 teaspoon Worchestershire sauce
Dash of Tabasco sauce
4 cups tomato juice

Combine all ingredients in a large glass bowl and chill for several hours before serving. This soup keeps well for days in the refrigerator, but the cayenne and Tabasco will get hotter as time goes by.

8 portions

ICY SPICY TOMATO SOUP

A zesty starter for grilled steaks or seafood.

28-ounce can Italian plum tomatoes in liquid
4 cups beef broth
1 1/2 cups grated celery root
1 clove garlic, minced
2 tablespoons fresh parsley, minced
1/2 teaspoon fresh dill, chopped
3/4 teaspoon fresh thyme, or 1/4 teaspoon dried
1/4 teaspoon ground celery seed
1/8 teaspoon crushed red pepper
Salt
Freshly ground pepper
1/2 teaspoon sugar

Garnish:
Sour cream
Fresh dill, finely chopped

Place all ingredients except the sour cream and dill in a large pot. Bring to a boil, cover, and simmer for 45-60 minutes, until the celery root is tender. Transfer to a blender or food processor and puree.

Chill in the refrigerator for several hours before serving. Top each bowl with a teaspoon of sour cream and a sprinkling of fresh dill.

6-8 portions

FRUITE SOUPE

"This is good for dessert. It can also be served with meat and it is delicious hot or cold. If I have company coming over after church for supper I serve this warm with flatbread as an appetizer," says Ruth Bakke, a full-blooded Norwegian and a renowned Skagit Valley cook.

1 pound prunes
1 pound raisins
2 quarts water
1 cup sugar
3 tablespoons quick tapioca
1 cup diced apples
3-4 cinnamon sticks
1 small lemon, sliced thin
1 small orange, sliced thin
1/2 cup blackberry or raspberry jam (optional)
Juice from one quart of canned apricots (reserve apricots)

Combine prunes, raisins, and water in a large saucepan. Simmer over medium heat for two hours. Add sugar, tapioca, apples, cinnamon sticks, lemon and orange slices, jam, and apricot juice. Cook, stirring occasionally, for 1/2 hour.

Stir in the reserved apricots and serve immediately, or chill for several hours in the refrigerator.

4-6 portions

CREAMY CARROT SOUP

Get a fresh start on summer suppers with this soup chilled, or feature it hot with roast chicken and biscuits for a cozy dinner.

2³/4 cups chicken broth
1 pound carrots (about 5), peeled and sliced
1 medium onion, cut into wedges
2 teaspoons curry powder
1 teaspoon fresh thyme
1 teaspoon freshly grated nutmeg
1 garlic clove, pressed
1 cup creme fraiche
¹/2 cup milk

Garnish: roasted filberts, sliced

In a large heavy saucepan, combine broth, carrots, onion, curry, thyme, nutmeg, and garlic. Cover and simmer over medium-low heat until vegetables are tender, about 15 minutes.

Puree soup in a blender or food processor. Return to saucepan and stir in creme fraiche and milk. Warm gently over low heat until heated through. Do not boil. Adjust quantity of milk to desired thickness.

Ladle into bowls and garnish with nuts. Serve hot or chilled.

4 portions

CURRIED PEA SOUP

Some like it hot, some like it cold. I like it both ways.

1 cup shelled peas, fresh or frozen
1 medium onion, sliced
2 carrots, sliced
1 medium potato, peeled and sliced
1 garlic clove
1 1/2 teaspoons curry powder
Salt
Freshly ground pepper
2 cups chicken stock
2/3 cup creme fraiche or buttermilk

In a large saucepan, combine peas, onion, carrots, potato, garlic, curry, salt, pepper, and 1 cup of chicken stock. Bring to a boil; reduce heat and simmer, covered, for 15 minutes.

Puree soup in blender or food processor. Pour into a large mixing bowl and add remaining chicken stock and creme fraiche. Whisk to blend well.

Chill well or reheat gently to serve.

6 portions

CREAM OF BROCCOLI SOUP

I always try to plan town trips on Thursdays so that I can lunch on a bowl of this beautiful smooth soup, a Thursday tradition at Judy Leber's Monkey Business cafe on Pine Street Plaza in Mount Vernon.

> *5 cups chicken stock*
> *5 cups chopped broccoli*
> *5 tablespoons butter*
> *$^1/_4$ cup all-purpose flour*
> *3 cups half-and-half*
> *Nutmeg*
> *Pepper*
> *Salt*

Steam broccoli in chicken stock until barely cooked. Let cool, then process mixture in a blender or food processor until finely chopped.

In a large saucepan, melt butter over low heat. Add flour and whisk to make a paste. Add half-and-half slowly, and cook for 10 minutes or so until slightly thickened. Add pureed broccoli. Season to taste with nutmeg, pepper, and salt.

CURRIED PUMPKIN SOUP

A perfect soup for fall harvest suppers or as a lovely beginning to the big roast turkey feast on Thanksgiving.

1/4 cup butter
1 large onion, sliced
3/4 cup green onion, sliced, white part only
2 cups pumpkin puree
4 cups chicken broth
1 bay leaf
1/2 teaspoon ginger
1/2 teaspoon curry powder
1/4 teaspoon nutmeg
Few fresh parsley sprigs
2 cups half-and-half
Salt
Freshly ground pepper

Garnish:
1/2 cup sour cream or yogurt
1/2 cup minced green onion or chives

Melt butter in a large saucepan over medium-high heat. Add onions and saute until soft and golden brown. Stir in pumpkin, chicken stock, bay leaf, ginger, curry powder, nutmeg, and parsley. Bring to a simmer, then reduce heat and continue simmering, uncovered, for 15 minutes.

Transfer soup in batches to blender or food processor and puree until smooth. Return to saucepan and add half-and-half. Add salt and pepper to taste. Simmer for 5 minutes, but do not allow to boil.

To serve hot, ladle into individual bowls. Float a dollop of sour cream on each and top with green onions or chives.

To serve cold, chill soup thoroughly, serve in individual bowls and garnish with sour cream and chives.

6 portions

HERBED LENTIL SOUP

Take the chill out of a rainy winter evening with this hearty soup and a big glass of Beaujolais.

8 ounces smoked, lean country bacon, coarsely chopped
2 large onions, diced
2 medium carrots, sliced
1/2 small cabbage, diced
2 garlic cloves, minced
2 bay leaves
1 tablespoon fresh marjoram, or 1 1/2 teaspoons dried
1 1/2 teaspoons fresh summer savory, or 1/2 teaspoon dried
1/2 teaspoon caraway seeds, coarsely ground
2 large fresh tomatoes, coarsely chopped
1/4 cup tomato paste
2 tablespoons sweet paprika
1/2-3/4 teaspoon chili powder
8-10 cups chicken stock
2 cups lentils
Salt
Freshly ground pepper

Garnish: 1 1/2 cups plain yogurt

Fry bacon in a large heavy saucepan over medium heat until crisp, stirring occasionally. Reserve 2 tablespoons of bacon grease and drain the rest. Add the onions, carrots, cabbage, garlic, bay leaves, marjoram, savory, and caraway seeds. Cover and cook over medium-low heat until vegetables are tender, about 20 minutes, stirring occasionally. Add tomatoes, tomato paste, paprika, and chili powder. Cook for 3 minutes, stirring constantly. Add 8 cups of chicken stock. Cover saucepan partially and simmer for 1 hour.

Add lentils, cover partially and simmer for 2 to 2 1/2 hours, stirring frequently and adding more stock if soup becomes too thick. Season to taste with salt and pepper and more chili pepper if you like. Simmer for 15 more minutes. Serve topped with a dollop of yogurt.

4-6 portions

Sensational
SALADS

CREAM OF THE CROP

Enjoy the freshest berries, apples, and cherries topped with a thick custard cream. I always try to make sure there will be enough left over for breakfast.

2 eggs
¹/₂ cup sugar
1 tablespoon all-purpose flour
Juice of 1 lemon, freshly squeezed
1 cup pineapple juice
1 pint whipping cream, whipped

2 pints fresh mixed fruit

In a heavy saucepan, mix the eggs, sugar, flour, lemon juice, and pineapple juice. Bring to a boil, and simmer until thickened, stirring constantly. Cool thoroughly, and fold in whipped cream.

Arrange berries and fruits in individual sherbet dishes. Spoon dressing over the top and garnish with a couple of fresh berries.

6-8 portions

SEASON'S BEST FRUIT SALAD

2 cups of a variety of fruits such as:
Raspberries
Green grapes
Pears
Peaches
Bananas
Blueberries
Strawberries
Kiwi fruit

DRESSING

2 tablespoons honey
2 tablespoons lime juice
2 tablespoons dark rum

Combine honey, lime juice, and rum. Pour over 2 cups of mixed sliced and chopped fruit and refrigerate for several hours. Serve in chilled cocktail glasses.

4 portions

ORANGE NASTURTIUM
SALAD

This dark green salad with orange sections and nasturtiums is a knockout.

1 head Romaine lettuce
1 head red leaf lettuce
12-24 nasturtium flowers, stemmed
2 oranges, peeled and sectioned
1 bunch green onions, chopped

ORANGE VINAIGRETTE

$^1/_2$ cup salad oil
$^1/_4$ cup fresh orange juice
$^1/_4$ cup rice vinegar
$^1/_2$ teaspoon soy sauce
1 onion, thinly sliced

Clean and dry the lettuce and tear leaves into a large salad bowl, or arrange on individual salad plates. Decorate with nasturium flowers and orange sections, and sprinkle with green onion slices.

Mix together ingredients for dressing and shake well. Drizzle dressing over salad and serve immediately.

6 portions

SHERRY VINAIGRETTE SALAD

A classic from the Oyster Bar.

Red leaf lettuce
Green leaf lettuce
Radicchio

SHERRY VINAIGRETTE

$1/4$ cup shallots, minced
$1/4$ cup sherry vinegar
$1/4$ cup champagne vinegar
$1/8$ cup Dijon mustard
$1/2$ cup virgin olive oil
$1/2$ cup corn oil
$1/4$ teaspoon salt
$1/4$ teaspoon pepper

To make vinaigrette, combine shallots, sherry vinegar, champagne vinegar, and mustard in a large bowl. Slowly add the olive oil and corn oil while whisking constantly. Salt and pepper to taste.

Serve over torn lettuce leaves.

BUTTER LETTUCE AND RASPBERRY SALAD

Patricia Hicks tossed in this tasty combo.

1-2 heads butter lettuce
1 cup fresh raspberries
$1/2$ cup dried apricots

RASPBERRY VINAIGRETTE

$3/4$ cup light olive oil
$1/4$ cup raspberry vinegar
Sugar
Salt
Freshly ground pepper

Combine butter lettuce, raspberries, and dried apricots in a salad bowl. In a separate bowl, combine oil and vinegar. Add sugar, salt, and pepper to taste. Stir or shake well, and pour sparingly over the lettuce and fruit just before serving.

CAESAR SALAD

One of our favorite suppers is this rich salad with lots of crusty chewy bread and a dry white wine.

2 heads Romaine lettuce, torn and chilled
1 cup freshly grated Parmesan cheese
1 cup fresh garlic croutons

DRESSING

³/₄ cup olive oil
¹/₄ cup fresh lemon juice
1 egg, lightly beaten
2-3 garlic cloves, pressed
1 teaspoon Worcestershire sauce
2-3 large anchovy fillets, chopped
Freshly ground pepper

In a large salad bowl, combine lettuce, cheese, and croutons.

In a jar, mix all dressing ingredients, and shake vigorously, blending well. Toss salad with dressing just before serving.

4 portions as a main course

SPINACH, APPLE, AND BACON SALAD

An unusual and inspired combination, lightly dressed with mustard.

1/4 pound bacon, cut into 2-inch slices
1 pound fresh spinach, torn
1 unpeeled red apple, coarsely chopped
3 green onions, sliced

MUSTARD DRESSING

1/4 cup olive oil
3 tablespoons red wine vinegar
1 teaspoon sugar
1 tablespoon prepared mustard
Salt
Freshly ground pepper

To make dressing, combine olive oil, vinegar, sugar, and mustard in a jar and shake well. Add salt and pepper to taste.

Fry bacon until crisp. Set aside to cool. In a salad bowl, combine spinach, apple, and onions. Crumble bacon over the top. Toss with dressing and serve.

6 portions

SPINACH AND SHRIMP SALAD

Every mouthful is a pleasant surprise.

1 large avocado, peeled and sliced into rings
1 tablespoon fresh orange juice
1 pound fresh spinach, torn into pieces
1 pound shrimp
3 oranges, sectioned

ORANGE DRESSING

²/₃ cup salad oil
¹/₃ cup freshly squeezed orange juice
2 tablespoons sugar
1 tablespoon red wine vinegar
¹/₂ teaspoon grated orange peel
¹/₄ teaspoon salt
¹/₄ teaspoon dry mustard
¹/₈ teaspoon hot pepper sauce

To make dressing, combine salad oil, ¹/₃ cup orange juice, sugar, vinegar, orange peel, salt, mustard, and hot pepper sauce in a jar. Shake well and chill.

Sprinkle avocado rings with 1 tablespoon of orange juice. Combine avocado, spinach, shrimp, and orange sections in a large salad bowl. Toss with chilled dressing.

8 portions

Skagit Valley spinach

SKAGIT SALAD

This makes a very appealing meal with French bread and cheap red wine.
I like to arrange it on salad plates as the heavier ingredients tend to drop
down to the bottom.

¹/₂ cup cashews
¹/₄ pound bacon, cut into bits
1 head fresh cauliflower
2 generous bunches fresh spinach

DIJON DRESSING

1 green onion, chopped
¹/₃ cup sugar
1 teaspoon celery seed
¹/₂ teaspoon freshly ground pepper
¹/₃ cup water
¹/₄ cup wine vinegar
2 tablespoons Dijon mustard
1 cup good salad oil

For dressing, mix onion, sugar, celery seed, pepper, water, vinegar,
mustard, and salad oil with wire whip or shake well in a jar.

If cashews are raw, toast them in a tablespooon or so of butter in an
iron skillet over medium heat until they are lightly browned.

Fry bacon bits until crisp.

Break the cauliflower into bite-sized flowerets and blanch in boiling
water for 1-2 minutes. Drain and cool.

Tear spinach into pieces, and combine in a large salad bowl or on
individual salad plates with cooled blanched cauliflower, bacon, and
cashews.

If using a salad bowl, toss with dressing just before serving. If arrang-
ing the salad on plates, drizzle with dressing and serve immediately.

4-6 portions

WILD MEADOW GREENS AND EDIBLE FLOWER SALAD

The Black Swan Cafe is renowned for this dramatic Northwoods salad. Be adventurous and create your own version at home.

GREENS

Select a combination of foraged greens such as:
Purple vetch
Dandelion
Shepherd's purse
Wild mustard
Chickweed
Wood sorrel
Lamb's quarters

RASPBERRY-MINT DRESSING

1/4 cup fresh mint (peppermint is best)
1 egg
1/2 cup raspberry vinegar
1/2 tablespoon honey
Dash salt
Dash white pepper
3/4 cup extra virgin olive oil

EDIBLE FLOWERS FOR GARNISH

Violas
Pansies
Forget-me-nots
Nasturiums
Wild mustard blossoms

Combine all dressing ingredients in a food processor or blender and blend well. Set aside.

Clean and chill selected greens. Arrange on individual salad plates or in a large salad bowl. Toss or drizzle with salad dressing and decorate with edible flowers.

COOL CUCUMBER SALAD

Cucumbers are to me the epitome of summer. This tangy and refreshing Oriental treatment comes from Grace H. Sakuma. She and her family farm over 500 acres of fruits and vegetables in the valley.

3 cups cucumbers, thinly sliced
1/2 teaspoon salt
1 teaspoon fresh ginger, finely chopped

RICE VINEGAR DRESSING

3/4 cup sweet cooking rice wine
1 cup Japanese rice vinegar
1 teaspoon salt

Combine dressing ingredients and bring to a boil. Set aside and cool thoroughly.

Partly peel cucumber, leaving strips of green. Slice very thin. Add salt to cucumbers and let stand for about 15 minutes. Press excess liquid from cucumbers, add the ginger and the dressing, and chill thoroughly before serving.

6 portions

PEA AND ALMOND SALAD

This salad is so easy and so satisfying that I use it for all sorts of occasions—it's a splendid addition to a holiday buffet, and a quick way to dress up a picnic in the boat.

10 ounces peas, fresh or frozen
6-ounce can smoked almonds
3 green onions, chopped
1/3 cup mayonnaise
1 tablespoon curry

If using fresh peas, shell and blanch for 3-5 minutes, until tender, yet firm. Drain and cool.

Combine peas, almonds, and green onion. Combine mayonnaise and curry, pour over peas and almonds, and toss well.

8 small portions

ONION AND GREEN BEAN SALAD

A flavorful departure from the ubiquitous green salad.

20 ounces fresh green beans
1 teaspoon salt
2 Walla Walla sweet onions (or any mild-flavored onion), sliced
1 tablespoon sugar
5 slices bacon
1/2 cup roasted filberts

DRESSING

1/3 cup olive oil
2 tablespoons white vinegar
1/2 teaspoon fresh basil, crushed
Dash cayenne pepper

Add the green beans and salt to 1 1/2 quarts of rapidly boiling water. Return to boiling and cook beans until just tender—about 15 minutes. Transfer to very cold water, and let cool completely. Drain thoroughly, and place in a medium salad bowl.

Separate onion slices into rings and place on top of beans. Sprinkle with sugar and toss well. Chill for at least one hour.

Fry bacon until crisp, crumble, and set aside.

To make dressing, combine olive oil, vinegar, basil, and cayenne in a small bowl. Blend well. Pour oil mixture over beans and onions, add the bacon and filberts, and toss gently.

6 portions

RED POTATO SALAD

Red leaf lettuce leaves
2 tomatoes, cut into wedges
2 hard boiled eggs, sliced
Fresh parsley, chopped

DRESSING

1 cup chicken stock
2 tablespoons minced onion
1 garlic clove, minced
1/4 cup olive oil
2 tablespoons champagne-wine vinegar
2 teaspoons tarragon leaves, crushed
1/4 teaspoon freshly ground black pepper
2 pounds small or tiny red potatoes, left whole or halved

Preheat oven to 350 degrees.

Heat chicken stock and combine with onion and garlic. Let stand for 10 minutes. Add oil, vinegar, tarragon, and black pepper.

Place potatoes in a shallow 7 1/2 X 12-inch baking dish. Pour dressing over all and toss to coat. Bake in oven for about 35-45 minutes, until potatoes are fork tender, stirring occasionally during baking. Most of the liquid will be absorbed.

Cool to room temperature. Arrange lettuce leaves on a large platter and top with potatoes, pouring any extra liquid over the top. Garnish with tomato wedges, hard-cooked egg slices and chopped parsley.

6 portions

PEPPER SALAD

Enjoy this colorful salad with a grilled steak and a well-chilled lager beer.

6 large red peppers
6 large green peppers
¹/₂ cup olive oil
4 tablespoons fresh lemon juice
¹/₂ teaspoon salt
Freshly ground pepper
2 tablespoons chopped fresh parsley
1 tablespoon chopped fresh basil

Preheat oven to 450 degrees.

Place peppers on baking sheet and roast until they are soft and their skins are black, about 30 minutes. Let cool slightly. Peel off skins and cut peppers into strips.

Combine oil, lemon juice, salt, and pepper in a deep bowl. Add peppers and toss gently until well-coated. Cover and marinate at room temperature for 1 to 2 hours.

This salad can be prepared ahead and marinated in the refrigerator for up to 24 hours. Bring it to room temperature and add parsley and basil just before serving.

8-12 portions

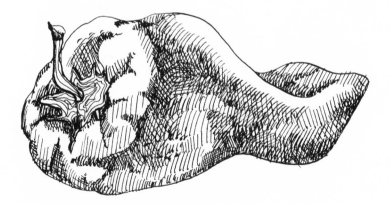

These fresh-flavored vinegars are great mixed with olive oil to dress green salads and bowls of fruit.

RASPBERRY WINE VINEGAR

2 cups fresh ripe raspberries
2 cups white wine vinegar

Pour vinegar over fruit in a large glass jar. Metal lids cause a reaction with the vinegar, so cover with plastic inside a lid or with a glass plate. Let stand for two to three weeks in a cool dark place. Strain well, heat but don't boil, and pour into clean glass bottles. Close tightly. If your berries are not sweet enough, a small amount of sugar may be added.

BLACKBERRY VINEGAR

4 pounds fresh blackberries
1 quart distilled white vinegar
Sugar

Sort and rinse berries and drain well. Using potato masher or hands, crush fruit in large bowl. Add vinegar and stir well. Pour into 1-gallon glass jar and cover tightly with a lid or with plastic wrap. Store in a cool, dark place for 3 to 4 weeks, stirring every other day.

Line a large ceramic bowl with a jelly bag or pillowcase. Pour in fruit and vinegar. Hang over bowl for several hours to allow juice to drain into bowl, but do not squeeze the bag.

Preheat oven to 300 degrees.

Discard drained fruit from bag. Measure vinegar. For every 2 cups of vinegar, place 3 tablespoons of sugar in large baking pan. Warm in oven for 8 to 10 minutes.

Meanwhile, pour vinegar into a pot large enough that vinegar stands no more than 4 inches deep. Otherwise, cook vinegar in batches. Place vinegar over high heat until warmed through. Stir in heated sugar and quickly bring to a boil. Boil for 3 minutes. Pour into a clean container and let stand overnight.

Carefully strain vinegar through cheesecloth into sterilized bottles. Cap or seal bottles and store in a cool, dark place until ready to use.

SUPPER
SALADS

Salade Niçoise

SALADE NICOISE

The fresh vegetables and shrimp lay artfully beneath a lattice of anchovies. This is a handsome salad for a Provencal buffet.

3/4 pound fresh green beans, cut into thirds
1 teaspoon salt
7 ounces drained shrimp
1 small or 1/2 large cucumber, peeled and thinly sliced
10 to 12 anchovy fillets, drained and split lengthwise
1/4 cup Italian black olives or Greek olives, halved and pitted
3 medium tomatoes, peeled, seeded, and cut into quarters

VINAIGRETTE

2 tablespoons fresh lemon juice
1 garlic clove, crushed
Salt
Freshly ground pepper
6 tablespoons olive oil

To make vinaigrette, combine lemon juice, garlic, salt, and pepper in a small bowl. Whisk in olive oil and set aside.

Add green beans and 1 teaspoon of salt to 1 quart of rapidly boiling water. Return to a boil and cook beans until just tender, about 15 minutes. With a slotted spoon, transfer beans to a basin of ice water and let cool completely. Drain thoroughly.

Place shrimp in a shallow serving dish or salad bowl. Cover with green beans and moisten with some of the vinaigrette. Cover beans with overlapping rows of cucumber slices. Spoon more vinaigrette over the cucumbers, reserving only a small amount.

Arrange anchovies in a lattice pattern on top of cucumbers. Put an olive half, rounded side up, in the center of each lattice. Arrange tomato wedges around the edge of the salad and brush with remaining vinaigrette. Cover and chill for up to 8 hours before serving.

6 portions

WILD RICE AND MUSSEL SALAD

Crunchy pine nuts and wild rice team up with tender mussels for a warm salad of outstanding character.

1/4 cup pine nuts
1 cup wild rice, well rinsed
1 1/2 teaspoons salt
6 tablespoons unsalted butter
2 medium shallots, minced
1/2 cup dry white wine
1 bouquet garni: 4 parsley stems, 1 bay leaf, 1/4 teaspoon thyme, tied
*   in a double thickness of cheesecloth*
3 pounds mussels, well scrubbed, beards removed
1 bunch scallions, thinly sliced
1/2 teaspoon ground pepper
4-6 large leaves butter lettuce

Preheat oven to 375 degrees.

Spread pine nuts in a small baking pan. Bake, shaking the pan occasionally, until the nuts are toasted and lightly browned, (3-4 minutes).

In a medium saucepan, combine rice, 1 teaspoon of salt, and 4 cups of cold water. Bring to a boil, then reduce to a simmer. Cover and cook for 25 minutes, until the rice is barely tender – still slightly chewy. Drain and set aside.

Meanwhile, melt 3 tablespoons of butter in a large skillet. Add shallots and saute until softened but not brown. Add wine, bouquet garni, and mussels. Increase the heat to high, cover and cook, shaking the pan occasionally, for about 3 minutes or until the mussels open. Remove from heat. Cool until the mussels can be handled. Remove them from their shells and place in a small bowl. Strain the cooking liquid into a saucepan and boil over high heat until it is reduced to 1/2 cup.

In a large saucepan, melt the remaining 3 tablespoons of butter. Add wild rice, scallions, and reduced mussel liquid. Toss. Add pepper, mussels, pine nuts, and remaining 1/2 teaspoon of salt. Cook, tossing constantly, for about 3 minutes, until warmed through.

Serve immediately, placing each serving on a leaf of lettuce.

4-6 servings

MIXED SEAFOOD SALAD WITH LEMON DRESSING

A well-known specialty from the Rhododendron Cafe. Enjoy with a big Chardonnay.

20 mussels
20 clams
1 tablespoon butter
1/8 teaspoon thyme
Pinch pepper
1/8 cup white wine
1 bayleaf
1/8 cup chopped onions

8 ounces fresh scallops
8 medium shrimp
1 cup water
1/2 cup white wine
1/4 teaspoon thyme
Salt
Freshly ground black pepper

1 green pepper, diced
1 red pepper, diced
1 stalk celery, diced
1/4 cup purple onion, diced
1 head Romaine lettuce
1 head green leaf lettuce

lemon juicer

LEMON DRESSING

1 cup mayonnaise
¹/₈ cup lemon juice
1 tablespoon dry mustard
Dash white pepper

Garnish:
Tomato wedges
Lemon wedges
Chopped parsley

Steam mussels and clams in a kettle with butter, thyme, pepper, white wine, bayleaf, and onions. Set aside.

Poach scallops and shrimp in water, wine, thyme, salt, and pepper. Set aside.

Blend together chopped vegetables and torn lettuces with lemon dressing. Arrange dressed lettuce and vegetables on four salad plates, top with seafood, and garnish with tomato and lemon wedges and chopped parsley.

4 portions

CURRIED CHICKEN SALAD

I never tire of this chicken salad. It makes a great standby for casual back-yard suppers and picnics.

3 chicken breast halves, cooked and torn into pieces
1 medium red onion, sliced
8 small new potatoes, cooked and quartered
1¹/₂ cups artichoke hearts, drained
¹/₂ head lettuce, chopped

CURRY DRESSING

¹/₂ cup mayonnaise
2 teaspoons curry powder

Mix dressing, using more or less curry to taste.

Combine chicken, onion, potatoes, and artichoke hearts in a salad bowl and toss with dressing. Serve over chopped lettuce.

4-6 portions

DUCK, ORANGE, AND FILBERT SALAD

Add a crusty bread and a Washington Chardonnay for a special fall meal.

4 duck breasts, skinned and sliced into ¹/₄-inch strips
2 tablespoons fresh lemon juice
1 teaspoon fresh tarragon
1 teaspoon fresh parsley

¹/₄ cup green onions, minced
3 tablespoons olive oil
2 tablespoons fresh lemon juice
Freshly ground pepper
Juice and grated peel of 1 orange

1 tablespoon butter
1 garlic clove
¹/₄ cup filberts, coarsely chopped

1 medium orange, thinly sliced
Romaine or Bibb lettuce leaves

In a small bowl, combine 2 tablespoons of lemon juice with tarragon and parsley. Arrange duck breasts in a shallow dish and brush lemon mixture over duck. Let stand at room temperature for 1 hour.

Preheat broiler.

Place duck in a broiling pan and broil until browned, turning once, for about 3 minutes per side.

In a medium bowl, combine green onion, oil, 2 tablespoons of lemon juice, orange juice and peel, and freshly ground pepper. Add broiled duck. Refrigerate for at least 2 hours, stirring occasionally.

Meanwhile, melt butter in a small skillet. Add garlic and cook for about 2 minutes over low heat. Discard garlic. Add the filberts and cook until browned and crisp, stirring frequently. Remove from heat and set aside.

To serve, add orange slices to the duck strips and toss well. Arrange lettuce leaves on individual plates. Spoon duck mixture over lettuce and sprinkle with filberts.

4-6 portions

PASTA PRIMA VERTE SALAD

Red, white, and green perk up this salad bowl.

1 pound fresh linguine or rotelle
10 ounces fresh blanched peas, or thawed frozen peas
1 pound fresh broccoli, cut into flowerets
1³/4-ounce can pimento, chopped
1¹/2 cups chopped fresh parsley
2 cups grated Parmesan cheese
1¹/2 cups half-and-half
1 teaspoon salt
¹/2 teaspoon white pepper

Cut linguine into 6-inch lengths or use rotelle. Cook for 2 minutes in boiling salted water. Do not overcook. Drain and rinse in cold water until cool.

Blanch broccoli in boiling water for 1-2 minutes. Drain well and combine in a large bowl with peas, pimento, parsley, and Parmesan cheese. Pour half-and-half over the top, add salt and pepper, and mix well.

Add vegetable misture to cooled pasta and toss well. Serve at room temperature and chill.

6 portions

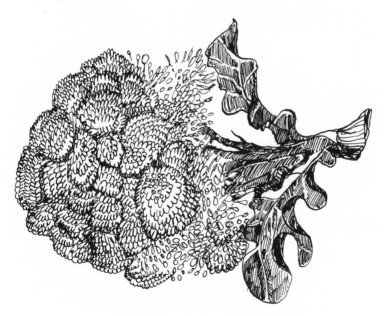

GREEK SALAD

2 tomatoes, cut in wedges
2 cucumbers, sliced
1 sweet white onion, sliced
1/2 cup Greek olives, sliced
1/2 pound feta cheese, crumbled
1 tablespoon fresh oregano
1/2 tablespoon fresh basil
2 cloves garlic, crushed
Freshly ground black pepper
1/4 cup fresh parsley, chopped
1 tablespoon fresh mint, chopped (optional)
1 cup olive oil
1/3 cup white wine vinegar
3 tablespoons fresh lemon juice

In a large salad bowl, combine tomatoes, cucumber, onion, Greek olives, feta cheese, oregano, basil, garlic, parsley, and pepper. Lightly dress with olive oil, then drizzle with vinegar and lemon juice.

Or colorfully arrange vegetables, olives, and feta on individual salad plates. Sprinkle with herbs and spices, then drizzle olive oil, vinegar, and lemon juice over each plate.

4 portions

VALLEY
Vegetables

POTATOES ROMANOFF

A memorable side dish with baked or grilled salmon.

6 medium potatoes, peeled
1 bunch green onions, chopped
1 1/2 cups shredded Cheddar cheese
1 pint sour cream
Salt
Freshly ground pepper
Paprika
More shredded Cheddar cheese

The night before serving, boil potatoes until fork tender. Grate potatoes and combine with green onions, Cheddar cheese, sour cream, salt, and pepper. Store in the refrigerator overnight in an ovenproof casserole.

Preheat oven to 350 degrees.

Cover top of casserole with more shredded Cheddar cheese and sprinkle with paprika.

Bake uncovered for 45-60 minutes, until lightly browned.

SESAME BROCCOLI

A nice accompaniment to Spiced Chicken Strips.

1 large bunch broccoli
1/2 cup sesame seeds, toasted
1/4 cup sake
1 1/2 tablespoons soy sauce
2 teaspoons sesame oil
2 teaspoons honey

Break broccoli into flowerets and peel and slice stems.

Drop broccoli into 2-3 quarts of boiling water. Cook until crisp-tender, about 6 to 8 minutes. Drain and cool to room temperature.

In a large bowl, combine sesame seeds, sake, soy sauce, sesame oil, and honey. Add broccoli and toss to mix well.

Serve immediately.

6 portions

STIR-FRIED CABBAGE WITH CARROTS

Cabbage seeds were one of the first commercial crops to meet success in the valley, beginning in the 1870s with the Tillinghast family. Their seed company is still a thriving landmark in LaConner, and the Skagit Valley is today a major world producer. Luckily, there are plenty of cabbages for eating, too.

> 1 tablespoon oil
> 1 small head cabbage
> 1 medium carrot, peeled
> 1/2 teaspoon salt
> 1/3 cup soup stock

Cut cabbage into quarters and slice into 1/2-inch slices. Cut carrot in half lengthwise, and slice into thin diagonal slices.

Heat wok and add oil. When oil is steaming hot, add cabbage, carrots, salt, and soup stock to wok, stirring together. Cover and cook for 1-2 minutes, or until vegetables are tender.

Serve immediately.

4 portions

A. G. Tillinghast threshing cabbage seed
La Conner — 1892.

EGGPLANT PARMAGINO

Oh, to be an eggplant and have purple skin!

1 medium eggplant
2 tablespoons peanut oil
¹/4 cup finely chopped onion
¹/4 cup finely chopped celery
¹/4 cup finely chopped green pepper
¹/2 cup grated Parmesan or sharp Gruyere cheese
2 medium tomatoes, peeled, with seeds removed
1 clove garlic, crushed
Dash salt
Dash black pepper

Preheat oven to 400 degrees.

Wash, dry, and slice eggplant into half-inch cross sections (5-8 slices). Blanch quickly in steamer for about 3-5 minutes. Drain and place evenly on oiled baking dish

Heat oil in frying pan. Add onions, celery, and green pepper, and saute until tender. Spoon onion mixture over eggplant slices. Make a second layer with grated cheese.

Puree tomatoes in blender and add garlic, salt, and pepper. Cover eggplant slices with puree.

Bake for 15 minutes until tops begin to brown. Serve at once.

6 portions

SPINACH TIMBALES

Even non-spinach eaters love this served at the Oyster Bar.

³/4 cup minced onion
¹/2 cup butter
1 cup sour cream
2²/3 cups cooked, drained, and chopped spinach
¹/4 teaspoon pepper
1¹/2 teaspoons salt
8 egg yolks

Preheat oven to 475 degrees.

Cook onions in butter until soft. Add sour cream, spinach, pepper, and salt. Mix well and allow to cool. Add egg yolks and blend well. Portion into individual timbale molds and bake for 20 minutes. Serve with Hollandaise sauce.

4-6 portions

MOUNTAIN SONG SPINACH QUICHE

An excellent spinach quiche from the Mountain Song Restaurant in Marblemount.

> 1 9-inch deep dish pastry shell
> 5 eggs
> 1 1/2 cups half-and-half
> 1/4 teaspoon dry mustard
> 1/8 teaspoon black pepper
> 1/16 teaspoon cayenne
> 1/8 teaspoon nutmeg
> 1/4 teaspoon salt
> 3/4 cup shredded Swiss cheese
> 1 cup onion, thinly sliced
> 1/2 cup mushrooms, sliced
> 1/2 pound fresh steamed spinach or frozen chopped spinach

Preheat oven to 375 degrees and prebake pie shell for 10 minutes. Set aside to cool.

Beat eggs lightly. Add half-and-half, mustard, pepper, cayenne, nutmeg, and salt. Blend well.

Spread shredded Swiss cheese on the bottom of pie shell. Add the onions, mushrooms, and well-drained spinach. Pour egg mixture over all. Bake for 45-60 minutes, until the middle is set. Remove from oven and let rest for 5 minutes before serving.

6 portions

GLAZED CARROTS

Enhanced only by pulling the carrots from your own garden.

> 2 pounds (about 10) carrots
> 6 tablespoons butter
> 1/2 cup sugar
> 1/2 teaspoon grated ginger

Peel carrots and cook until they are fork tender. Drain.

Melt butter in a small saucepan. Add sugar and ginger. Blend well and heat thoroughly. Add carrots and toss until they are completely coated. Transfer to a warm serving dish and serve immediately.

8 portions

SPINACH-STUFFED TOMATOES

These savory tomatoes are delicious served with lamb.

> *6 firm ripe tomatoes*
> *Salt*
> *1/4 cup olive oil*
> *5 green onions, coarsely chopped*
> *10 ounces (1 large bunch) fresh spinach, coarsely chopped*
> *1/4 cup fresh parsley, chopped*
> *1/4 cup fresh dill, chopped*
> *Freshly ground pepper*
> *1/2 cup crumbled feta cheese*

Slice 1/2 inch from the top of each tomato. Scoop out the pulp and seeds; chop pulp and reserve. Lightly salt tomato cavities and let drain upside down on paper towels.

Heat oil in a large skillet. Add onion and saute until tender. Add tomato pulp, spinach, parsley, dill, and pepper. Cook uncovered over high heat until most of liquid is absorbed, about 5 minutes. Remove from heat and stir in all but 2 tablespoons of cheese. Set aside to cool.

Preheat oven to 375 degrees.

Lightly oil a large baking dish. Divide stuffing among tomato shells, filling lightly. Sprinkle with remaining feta.

Place stuffed tomatoes in dish and bake until they are cooked through but not splitting, about 20 minutes.

6 portions

SQUASH EMPANADAS

Empanadas are Mexican turnovers, often stuffed with meat or vegetables or fruit. Anita Guillen recommends filling them with fresh ripe squash in the fall.

EMPANADAS

3 1/2 cups all-purpose flour
3 tablespoons brown sugar
1 tablespoon ground cinnamon
1 tablespoon ground aniseed
1 cup shortening
1 cup milk
2 egg yolks

Combine flour, sugar, and spices in a large mixing bowl. Cut in shortening with a pastry blender until mixture resembles coarse corn meal. Mix egg yolks into the milk and add to flour mixture. Work liquid in with a pastry blender until dough forms, then gather dough and press it firmly into a ball. Wrap in foil and refrigerate for 2 hours.

Preheat oven to 400 degrees.

Divide the dough into 24 small round pieces. Roll out each piece into a 4-inch circle. Place 2 tablespoons of Squash Filling on one half of each round and fold the other half over. Press the edges firmly to seal in the filling.

Bake for 20 minutes.

SQUASH FILLING

5 pounds winter squash
2 tablespoons ground cinnamon
2 cups brown sugar
2 tablespoons aniseed

Preheat oven to 375 degrees.

Cut squash into pieces and remove seeds and peel. Place pieces in a deep baking dish and bake, covered, for 45 minutes. Remove from oven and mix in sugar and spices with a potato masher. Return to oven and bake for 30 more minutes. Squash should be dry; if it is too liquid, stir over heat until excess moisture is evaporated.

PASTA,
Please

MY KITCHEN'S EGG PASTA DOUGH

3¹/₂ cups sifted all-purpose flour
5 eggs
1 tablespoon olive oil
1 teaspoon salt

Mound flour in a large open bowl and make a well in the center. In a medium bowl, beat eggs with oil and salt. Pour egg mixture into center of flour well, and work into flour with hands. Turn out onto floured board and knead until firm and smooth. Wrap ball of dough in a teacloth which has been wrung out in warm water and let rest for 30 minutes. Roll out dough for pasta intended.

FETTUCINE CARBONARA

Quick and easy and quite elegant.

¹/₄ pound bacon
1 egg
³/₄ cup Parmesan cheese, grated
1 cup heavy cream
¹/₄ cup butter, cut into pieces
2 garlic cloves, pressed
2 tablespoons chopped parsley
1 teaspoon salt
¹/₄ teaspoon freshly ground pepper
1 pound fettucine

Garnish: Fresh parsley, minced

Fry bacon until crisp, crumble, and set aside, keeping warm.
Beat the egg and add the Parmesan cheese, cream, butter, garlic, parsley, and salt and pepper.
Cook the pasta al dente, drain, and toss immediately with egg and cheese mixture. Sprinkle with crisp bacon and fresh parsley.
Serve on warm plates.

4 portions

FETTUCINE ALLA VONGOLE

Sweet clams!

2 tablespoons butter
2 cloves garlic, pressed
3 tablespoons flour
16 ounces chopped clams with juice
Salt
Freshly ground black pepper
1 teaspoon sweet basil
1/2 teaspoon thyme
1 cup whipping cream
1/2 cup Parmesan cheese, grated
1 tablespoon olive oil
1 pound fettucine noodles
1 tablespoon butter

Garnish:
Fresh parsley, chopped
Parmesan cheese, grated

In a heavy skillet, melt 2 tablespoons of butter. Add garlic and cook for 1 minute. Whisk in flour. Add clams and juice and combine well. Add salt and pepper to taste. Stir in basil, thyme, cream, and Parmesan cheese. Cook until hot, but do not boil.

Meanwhile, add salt and olive oil to a large pot of boiling water. Add pasta and cook al dente. Drain pasta and mix with 1 tablespoon of butter. Toss with clam sauce, and sprinkle fresh parsley and grated Parmesan on top.

4 portions

KING SALMON WITH PESTO

Big beautiful catch of the day from the Rhododendron Cafe. This dish seems complicated, but if the pesto and pasta are made ahead, there are only a few steps when dinner is to be served.

Fresh or dried egg pasta
24 ounces or 16 slices salmon filleted in 1/2-inch slices
Flour
1/4 cup butter
1/4 cup white wine
3/4 cup pesto
1 cup whipping cream

Garnish:
Parmesan cheese, grated
Parsley, chopped

FRESH EGG PASTA

4 cups semolina flour
1 cup all-purpose flour
1 1/2 teaspoons salt
7 large eggs
3 tablespoons olive oil

This dough can be made by hand in a large bowl or mixed in a food processor. Blend semolina flour and all-purpose flour with salt. Break in eggs and add olive oil. Mix briefly until well blended, then turn onto floured board or counter and knead for 2 minutes, until smooth and elastic. Divide the dough into 3-inch diameter balls, and wrap and refrigerate. If using a pasta machine, roll out and cut the fettucine noodles. Otherwise, roll dough out by hand into a thin sheet. Flour generously and gently fold sheet into a roll and cut 1/4-inch slices into noodles.

PESTO

1 packed cup fresh basil leaves, washed and spun dry
2 cloves garlic, chopped
1/4 cup chopped walnuts
1/5 cup pine nuts
1/2 cup olive oil
1/3 cup Parmesan cheese

In a food processor or blender, whirl basil, garlic, walnuts, and pine nuts until almost smooth. Add olive oil and Parmesan cheese slowly with machine running and blend well. Set aside until ready to use.

TO ASSEMBLE DINNER:

Add ¼ teaspoon of salt and 1 tablespoon of olive oil to 3 quarts of water and bring to a boil.

Lightly flour salmon slices. Melt butter in saute pan on low heat and add salmon slices when butter bubbles. Sprinkle lightly with salt and pepper. Turn salmon after about 30 seconds and add white wine, pesto, and cream. Gently blend together.

Add the pasta to water and cook about 2-3 minutes for fresh pasta. Allow about 6-8 minutes for dried pasta.

Check doneness of salmon and remove to a warmed plate. While sauce in pan reduces slightly until light and creamy instead of liquidy, assemble pasta and salmon. Distribute pasta evenly in either a large shallow serving bowl or on individual serving plates. Arrange salmon nicely on top of pasta. Pour sauce over salmon and pasta. Garnish with grated Parmesan and chopped parsley, and serve immediately.

4 portions

SHRIMP AND SCALLOP FETTUCINE

Here the shrimp and scallops are complemented by fresh asparagus and peas.

3/4 cup butter
3 garlic cloves, minced or pressed
1 cup sliced fresh asparagus
1/2 cup fresh peas
1/2 cup sliced green onion
1/2 pound pink shrimp, shelled and deveined
1/2 pound bay scallops
2 tablespoons parsley, minced
1 teaspoon basil, crushed
1/4 cup dry white wine
3/4 pound fettucine noodles, cooked and drained
Salt
Freshly ground pepper

Garnish: Parmesan cheese, grated

Melt butter in a large skillet or saucepan, and saute garlic. Add the asparagus, peas, and green onions; cook, stirring often, until vegetables are crisp-tender, about 5 minutes. Stir in shrimp, scallops, parsley, basil, and wine. Cook over high heat for 2 minutes, stirring constantly, until seafood is thoroughly heated. Add salt and pepper to taste.

Serve over hot fettucine, and sprinkle with Parmesan cheese.

6 portions

FISH
FINS

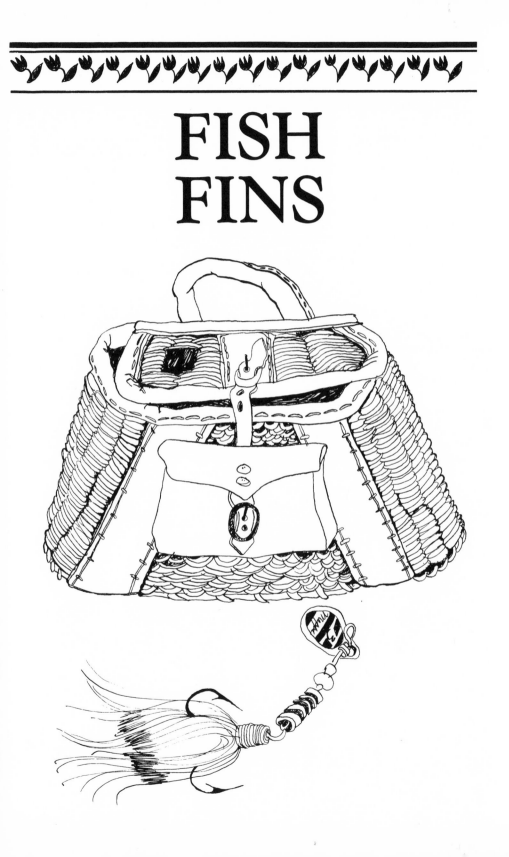

SALMON MOUSSE

Serve for an airy summer luncheon, or spread on toasts and crackers for a light first course.

1 envelope unflavored gelatin
2 tablespoons lemon juice
1 small onion, sliced
1/2 cup boiling water
1/2 cup mayonnaise
1/2 teaspoon paprika
2 teaspoons fresh dill
1 pound canned pink salmon, drained, or fresh poached salmon, skin
  and bones removed
1 cup heavy cream

Garnish: Fresh parsley

Place gelatin, lemon juice, onion, and water in blender and blend at high speed until onion is pureed. Add mayonnaise, paprika, dill, and salmon and blend again. Add cream, 1/3 cup at a time, and blend until very smooth.

Pour into 1-quart mold and chill overnight. To unmold, dip bottom and sides of mold into warm water and invert onto a serving platter. Decorate with parsley.

8 portions

SMOKED SALMON QUICHE

Linda Freed shares the recipe for this memorable quiche from The Calico Cupboard.

1 9-inch pie shell

3 tablespoons butter
1/3 cup finely chopped onion
4 large eggs
3/4 cup whipping cream
3/4 cup half-and-half
1/4 teaspoon salt
Dash cayenne
1/4 teaspoon dill weed
1 cup grated Swiss cheese
3/4 pound smoked salmon, boned and crumbled

Preheat oven to 400 degrees.

Melt butter and saute onion until soft. Beat eggs lightly. Combine onion and butter mixture with eggs, and add cream and half-and-half. Stir in salt, cayenne, and dill weed, and blend well.

Spread cheese and salmon in bottom of pie shell. Cover with egg mixture and bake until puffy and set, approximately 35 minutes. Cool on wire rack for 5-10 minutes before slicing.

6 portions

SALMON ON THE GREEN

Serve this lovely poached salmon when you have basil growing in the backyard.

Olive oil
1 1/2-pound salmon fillet
1/3 cup fresh lime juice
Freshly ground pepper

2 pounds salmon bones
3 celery stalks with leaves
1 medium carrot
4 parsley sprigs
2 thyme sprigs
1 large bay leaf
6 cups water
2 tablespoons butter
2 tablespoons flour
2 tablespoons whipping cream
1 teaspoon fresh lemon juice
1 cup fresh basil leaves

Garnish: 4 lime halves

Lightly oil a 9 X 12-inch baking dish. Skin the salmon and reserve the skin. Remove any small bones from the fillet and cut on the diagonal into 1/8-inch slices. Arrange slices in baking dish, and pour lime juice over. Sprinkle with pepper. Press waxed paper over the salmon strips and refrigerate for 8 hours.

In a large heavy saucepan, combine reserved salmon skin, bones, celery, carrot, parsley, thyme, and bay leaf. Add water and bring to a boil. Reduce heat and simmer until reduced by half, about 2 1/2 hours. Strain liquid into a fish poacher through several layers of dampened cheesecloth. Reserve 1 cup of this stock.

In a small heavy saucepan over low heat, melt 1 tablespoon of butter. Whisk in flour and stir for 3 minutes. Whisk in the cup of strained stock and bring to a boil. Reduce heat and simmer until reduced by one fourth, about 10 minutes. Whisk in cream, then lemon juice, and simmer for about 2 minutes. Whisk in the second tablespoon of butter. Pour into blender. Add fresh basil and puree until smooth. Return sauce to pan. If a thinner consistency is desired, add more fish stock.

Reheat remaining fish stock in poacher. Place salmon on lightly oiled rack of poacher. Place rack in poacher with enough stock to cover salmon and simmer over low heat until the salmon is just barely opaque, about 3-5 minutes.

To serve, spoon warm sauce onto heated serving plates. Using slotted spatula, transfer salmon slices to the center of each plate. Garnish with lime halves and serve.

4 portions

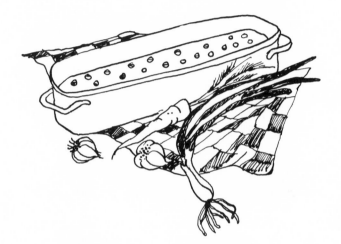

SAVORY SALMON KABOBS

A colorful surprise for a barbecue.

> *1 1/2 pounds salmon steaks*
> *1 medium zucchini*
> *1 dozen mushrooms*
> *1 dozen cherry tomatoes*

Remove skin and bones from salmon, and cut into sixteen 1 1/2-inch chunks. Alternate salmon, thick zucchini slices, mushrooms, and tomatoes on each of four skewers. Brush with lime butter. Place on grill about six inches about hot coals. Grill for about 8 minutes on the first side. Turn and baste with lime butter. Continue grilling until salmon flakes easily when tested with a fork (about another 8 minutes).

LIME BUTTER BASTING SAUCE

> *1/4 cup butter, melted*
> *2 tablespoons lime juice*
> *1 1/2 teaspoons finely chopped onion*
> *1 clove garlic, pressed*
> *1/4 teaspoon salt*
> *1/4 teaspoon thyme*
> *Dash black pepper*

4 portions

ALICE BAY
BARBECUED SALMON

This is a simple and delicious way to serve either salmon, halibut, or steelhead for a backyard picnic on a summer evening. I allow one-third pound of steaks or fillets per person and one-half pound of dressed fish per person.

Fish fillets, steaks, or dressed fish, at least 3/4 inch thick

BARBECUE SAUCE

1 cup butter
3 large cloves garlic, minced
4 tablespoons soy sauce
2 tablespoons mustard
1/4 cup catsup
Dash Worcestershire sauce

Mix all ingredients for barbecue sauce together in a saucepan and heat over medium heat.

Adjust grill so that it is 4-5 inches above coals. Grease grill and center fish over the coals. Baste generously with barbecue sauce. Grill, turning once, until the fish flakes easily when tested in the thickest portion with a fork. For fish 1 inch thick, I allow about 10 minutes total cooking time. When fish tests done, transfer to a warm serving platter. Garnish with lemon wedges and serve warm barbecue sauce on the side.

SALMON AND ASPARAGUS LOAF

A savory spring entree from the pantry before fishing season begins.

1 small bunch fresh asparagus
3 tablespoons butter
3 tablespoons all-purpose flour
¹/₂ teaspoon dillweed
1 tablespoon grated onion
¹/₈ teaspoon salt
1 cup chicken broth
1 pint of canned salmon
1¹/₂ cups cooked rice
3 eggs, slightly beaten

Preheat oven to 350 degrees.

Steam asparagus lightly and set aside.

Melt butter in a large saucepan. Stir in flour, dill, onion, and salt. Add chicken broth. Cook and stir until mixture thickens and bubbles. Stir in salmon, rice, and eggs.

Lay asparagus in bottom of a greased loaf pan. Press salmon mixture on top, and bake for 50 to 55 minutes. Invert loaf onto a serving platter and slice.

Serve with a Bechamel sauce.

BECHAMEL SAUCE

2 tablespoons butter
3 tablespoons all-purpose flour
2 cups heated milk
Salt
Freshly ground pepper

In a heavy saucepan, melt butter over low heat. Blend in flour and cook slowly, stirring constantly, for 2 minutes. Remove roux from heat. Gradually blend milk into roux with a wire whip until smooth. Return to medium heat and continue stirring until the sauce thickens and boils. Boil for 1 minute, stirring constantly. Add salt and pepper to taste.

6-8 portions

SILVER-LINED CANNED SALMON

In turn-of-the-century Anacortes, salmon canneries lined the waterfront, and cases of tins were shipped all over the world. Hundreds of Chinese workers were imported to clean and pack the fish, which poured in from May to October. These days we run our own cannery here in our Alice Bay kitchen when the salmon are at their peak.

Fillet a fresh salmon, leaving the skin on. Rinse and pat dry. Cut into pieces and pack into sterile pint canning jars to within 1 inch of top. Add $1/8$ teaspoon of salt and 1 tablespoon of olive oil. Wipe rims of jars.

Adjust hot, sterile, lids. Process for 100 minutes at 10 pounds pressure, with an appropriate amount of water for the capacity of your canner. (See instructions supplied with canner).

Canned salmon label.
1910.

TO FILLET A COD

I like to spend a lazy afternoon jigging for rock cod from our 12' sailing dory or spearfishing for Larry Ling Cod 40 feet below. Then there's filleting the fresh fish.

With the knife at a slight angle, make the first cut at the base of the head, moving towards the head. Cut to the backbone, but not through it.

Then turn the knife toward the tail, keeping the blade along the backbone. Advance the knife through the fish to the tail, cutting through the rib bones and just above the back bone.

With the fillet still attached to the tail, place the fillet skin side down. To skin the fillet, hold on to the tail of the fish. Make a small cut about 1/2 inch above the tail. Turn the knife at a slight angle and draw the fish along the knife, separating the first fillet. Cut the rib bones from the fillet. Turn the fish and repeat the procedure.

Your first attempt may not be a great success. The method is simple, but it may take a few Larry Lingcods to get the hang of it.

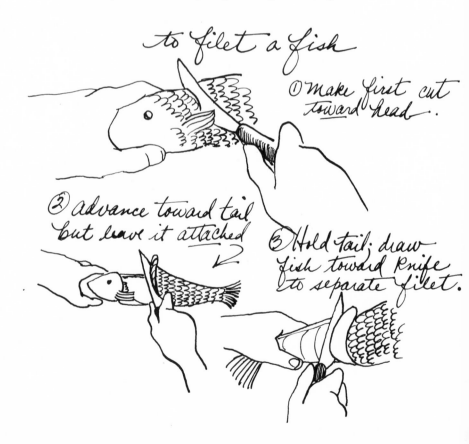

ROQUEFORT AND
SHRIMP-STUFFED COD

The Roquefort accents the cod beautifully, and fresh sliced tomatoes make an ideal side dish.

1 cup butter, softened
4 ounces cream cheese, at room temperature
6 ounces raw shrimp, cut into small pieces
6 ounces Roquefort cheese
2 tablespoons lemon juice
1 teaspoon chopped parsley
1 teaspoon chopped chives
1 green onion, minced
1/8 teaspoon hot pepper sauce
1/8 teaspoon Worcestershire sauce
Salt
Freshly ground pepper

3–4 pounds cod or rockfish fillets
1/2 cup butter, melted
1 cup seasoned bread crumbs

Combine butter, cream cheese, shrimp, Roquefort, lemon juice, parsley, chives, green onion, pepper sauce, and Worcestershire sauce. Add salt and pepper to taste.

Pat fish dry. Spread about 1/4 cup of the cheese filling on the skin side of each fillet. Roll fillets. Chill thoroughly, about 30 minutes.

Preheat oven to 375 degrees.

Dip each fillet into melted butter and roll in bread crumbs. Place in a shallow buttered baking dish, and drizzle with melted butter. Bake for approximately 20 minutes, or until the fish is white and flaky. Do not overcook. Check frequently after 15 minutes.

8 portions

COD CREOLE

Bubbling with flavor.

> *3/4 cup butter*
> *2 large onions, thinly sliced*
> *6 cups chopped green pepper*
> *6 cups chopped celery*
> *2 cloves fresh garlic, minced*
> *Salt*
> *Freshly ground pepper*
> *4 cups peeled and seeded chopped tomatoes*
> *1/2 cup chopped fresh parsley*
> *4 tablespoons drained capers*
> *Hot pepper sauce*
> *31/2 pounds codfish fillets, cut into serving pieces*

Melt butter in a large skillet over medium heat. Add onion and saute until tender. Add green pepper, celery, garlic, salt and pepper and saute briefly. Blend in tomato, parsley, and capers. Add hot pepper sauce to taste. Cover and cook for 15 minutes, then uncover and cook for 5 more minutes.

Preheat oven to 450 degrees.

Butter a large baking dish. Arrange cod fillets in dish and cover with sauce. Bake until fish flakes when fork-tested, about 15 minutes.

8-12 portions

FISH PLAKI

This robust baked fish needs only a green salad, crusty bread, and a chilled bottle of Demestica, a light Grecian wine.

2 pounds cod or halibut fillets
Salt
Freshly ground pepper
2 tablespoons fresh oregano
1/2 cup olive oil
3 large fresh tomatoes, sliced
3 scallions, chopped
1 cup fresh parsley, chopped
1 clove garlic, finely minced
2 large onions, thinly sliced into rings
2-3 lemons, sliced
1 cup water

Preheat oven to 350 degrees.

Place fish in a greased baking pan. Sprinkle with salt, pepper, and fresh oregano.

Heat olive oil in a frying pan. Lightly saute tomatoes, scallions, parsley, and garlic for about 3 minutes. Spread on top of fish and dot with butter. Arrange onion rings and lemon slices on top. Add water.

Bake for 25-30 minutes, testing for doneness, until the fish is opaque in color and flakes with a fork.

6 portions

HALIBUT WITH FRESH TOMATO SAUCE

A Provencal treatment of a fine Northwest fish. This fresh tomato sauce also poaches a salmon beautifully. Just add a little more liquid if needed.

> *2 pounds halibut steaks or fillets, 3/4 inch thick*
> *3/4 cup olive oil*
> *3 large tomatoes, peeled and coarsely chopped*
> *6 tablespoons red wine vinegar*
> *4 garlic cloves, minced*
> *2 tablespoons fresh rosemary*
> *3 teaspoons fresh thyme*
> *3 bay leaves*
> *Salt*
> *Freshly ground pepper*

In a heavy skillet, heat $1/2$ cup of olive oil over medium heat. Add fish in batches and fry until just opaque, about 2 minutes per side. Drain on paper towels.

Add $1/4$ cup of olive oil to skillet. Stir in tomatoes, vinegar, garlic, rosemary, thyme, and bay leaves. Add salt and pepper to taste. Simmer until liquid evaporates and sauce thickens, stirring frequently, about 15 minutes.

Arrange fish on platter. Top with sauce and cool. Garnish with bay leaves. Serve at room temperature.

8 portions

FRESH HALIBUT WITH RHUBARB SAUCE

The Black Swan donates this intriquing combination. They suggest Mount Baker Vineyards Muller Thurgau for the cooking wine...then enjoy the rest with the meal.

2 8-ounce halibut fillets
1 cup fish stock or water
1 Walla Walla sweet onion, chopped
1/2 cup white wine
1 tablespoon butter
1 teaspoon garlic, crushed
2 stalks fresh rhubarb, chopped
1 tablespoon strawberry vinegar
4 tablespoons creme fraiche or sour cream

Poach halibut fillets in fish stock or water with onion, wine, butter, and garlic. Remove fish from stock and keep warm. Add rhubarb and vinegar to the stock. Simmer until rhubarb is completely tender, about 5 minutes.

Force sauce through a food mill or strainer. Add creme fraiche or sour cream and blend well.

Cover bottom of serving dish with sauce and place halibut on top. Serve with extra sauce on the side.

4 portions

COLD POACHED STEELHEAD WITH SPINACH SAUCE

Perfect for a summer buffet, with fresh garden salads and a nice chilled Chardonnay.

> *1 steelhead, scaled, rinsed and patted dry*
> *1 quart water*
> *2 cups white wine*
> *2 carrots, chopped*
> *1/2 onion, chopped*
> *1/2 lemon, studded with cloves*
> *2 or 3 bay leaves*
> *Celery leaves*
> *2 sprigs parsley*
> *1 tablespoon salt*

In poacher or roasting pan, combine water, wine, carrots, onion, lemon, bay leaves, celery leaves, parsley and salt. Bring to a boil.

Lightly oil rack of poacher. Set prepared fish on rack and lower into liquid in poacher. Bring back to a boil. Lower heat and simmer for 10 minutes per inch, measured at the thickest part of fish.

Remove fish from poacher and gently transfer to a serving platter. Chill and serve with spinach sauce.

GREEN SPINACH SAUCE

> *3 shallots, chopped*
> *3/4 cup spinach, chopped*
> *3 tablespoons lemon juice*
> *2 tablespoons light vinegar, such as raspberry or pear*
> *2/3 cup walnut oil*
> *Salt*
> *White pepper, finely ground*
> *White wine, to thin*

Chop shallots and spinach, separately in food processor or by hand. Mix in a blender or food processor with lemon juice and vinegar. Add walnut oil slowly while vegetables are blending. Season with salt and pepper. Transfer to a bowl and use white wine to thin to desired pouring consistency.

8-10 portions

TROUT ORLEANS

A pretty and exotic entree.

2 fresh or fresh frozen trout
1-2 eggs
1 1/2 cups Japanese crumbs for breading
Unsalted butter
2 bananas, sliced lengthwise
1 large lemon, thinly sliced
1 large tomato, thinly sliced
Hollandaise sauce

Garnish: 1/2 cup chopped green onions

Clean and fillet trout. Beat eggs for coating fish in a large container. Place bread crumbs in another dish. Give the fish an egg wash and then dip in crumbs, coating each side. Melt enough butter in a large saute pan to brown fish. Saute fish, skin side down, for about 3 minutes. Turn fish, and add bananas on either side; saute for 3-5 minutes. Place alternating slices of lemon and tomato on top of fish. Run under broiler briefly.

Place fish on plate with bananas on either side. Cover with Hollandaise sauce and sprinkle with green onions.

HOLLANDAISE SAUCE

1 cup unsalted butter
3 egg yolks
1 tablespoon fresh lemon juice
Pinch salt
Pinch white pepper

Melt butter over low heat. Whirl eggs in blender or food processor until pale yellow. With blender/processor on low, slowly add butter in a slow stream, then lemon juice and salt and pepper to taste.

2-4 portions

TROUT WITH HAZELNUTS AND WILD BLACKBERRY SAUCE

Celebrate the long days of summer with fresh trout and blackberries, courtesy of The Oyster Bar.

>1 fresh trout
>$1/2$ cup coarsely chopped hazelnuts
>$1/2$ cup fresh bread crumbs
>Clarified butter

Fillet the trout and coat it in a mixture of hazelnuts and bread-crumbs. Saute in clarified butter until done, and top with blackberry sauce.

WILD BLACKBERRY BEURRE BLANC

>$1^1/2$ ounces red wine vinegar
>$1^1/2$ ounces white wine
>$1/4$ cup minced shallots
>$1/8$ teaspoon white pepper
>$1^1/2$ cups butter, chilled
>$1/2$ cup fresh, wild blackberries

Combine vinegar, wine, shallots, and pepper. Heat and reduce to 2 tablespoons. Slowly add butter, whisking constantly. Add blackberries, whisking and mashing the berries. Strain and serve over trout.

1 portion

SOLVANA TROUT

A recipe borrowed from Mount Baker Vineyards and enjoyed with their lovely Gewurztraminer.

1 pound trout (salmon or snapper)
1/4 cup butter
2 cloves garlic
1/2 teaspoon thyme
1/2 teaspoon rosemary
1/2 teaspoon sage
Dash freshly ground black pepper
1 cup sliced onions
1 cup sliced mushrooms
2 tablespoons lemon juice
1/4 cup Gewurztraminer wine
1/2 cup sour cream
1 cup choppped spinach
1/2 cup slivered almonds

Garnish:
2 fresh tomatoes, quartered
2 fresh lemons, cut in wedges

Melt butter in a large frying pan. Slice garlic and saute for 1 minute. Lightly saute herbs, pepper, onions, and mushrooms. Add fish, lemon juice, and wine, and allow to simmer for 5 minutes. Turn fish. Combine sour cream and spinach; spoon on top of fish. Sprinkle with almonds and allow cream mixture to heat thoroughly.

Garnish with tomatoes and serve with lemon wedges.

4 portions

SEA
SHELLS

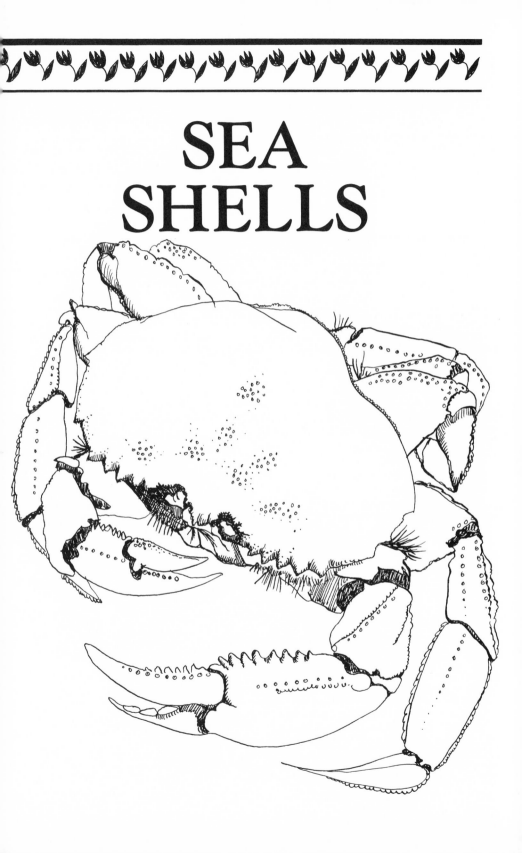

OYSTERS GALORE

An ice-cold tiny raw oyster, maybe with a squeeze of lemon, and you taste the fresh essence of the sea.

The Pacific oysters which are grown commercially here are not native to these waters, but were introduced from Japan. These mollusks are harvested by three companies, all within the skip of a stone for those of us on Samish Island. The Blau Oyster Company has been growing Pacific oysters in Samish Bay since 1935. Acme Oyster Company is run by Dave Von Allmon and Dave Schimke, who became the National Oyster Shucker when he shucked twenty-four oysters in less than three minutes. Just across the bay on Chuckanut Drive is the Rockpoint Oyster Company.

We gather our own oysters at Alice Bay and never tire of them. We eat them both raw and richly sauced, and we're always experimenting.

TO SHUCK AN OYSTER

The two shells are hinged together. The upper shell is fairly flat and the lower is cupped. Oysters should be handled with the lower, cupped, side down, in order to keep the liquor from spilling out, whether shucking or grilling them.

In shucking, the two-edged oyster knife is your tool. Insert the blade between the shells, about two-thirds of the way along the side from the hinged end of the shell. Move the knife back and forth horizontally against the inside of the top shell, cutting the adductor muscle. The shell will open, revealing the succulent oyster cupped in its own liquor.

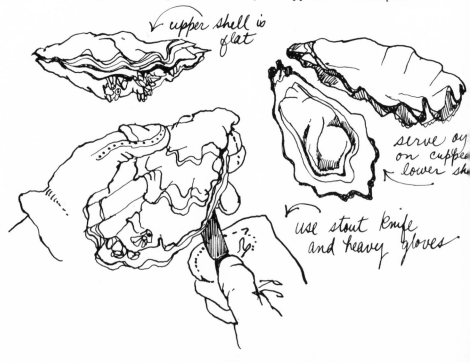

upper shell is flat

serve oy on cuppe lower sh

use stout knife and heavy gloves

OYSTER PIE

A wonderful entree for breakfast, lunch, or a light supper, compliments of the Mountain Song Restaurant.

1 single pie crust recipe
$1/3$ cup butter
$1/4$ cup onions, finely chopped
$1 1/3$ cup oysters, chopped
1 cup cooked potato, cubed
4 slices bacon, cooked, drained, and crumbled
Salt
Freshly ground pepper

Roll pie crust flat and cut into four pieces shaped to cover individual ramekins. Bake crusts on cookie sheet until brown. Set aside.

Melt butter in a large skillet. Saute onion until soft. Add oysters and saute briefly until edges curl. Add potato and bacon until heated through. Add salt and pepper to taste. Spoon mixture into four single-serving ramekins and cover each with a prebaked crust.

Pour mushroom sauce over crusts and serve hot. Garnish with sprigs of fresh parsley.

MUSHROOM SAUCE

2 tablespoons butter
3 tablespoons flour
2 cups water
$1/2$ teaspoon chicken boullion
1 tablespoon sherry
$1/2$ teaspoon salt
5 ounces fresh mushrooms, sliced and sauteed in butter

Melt butter in a saucepan or large skillet. Add flour and stir until smooth. Add water and boil for 3 minutes, stirring constantly. Add chicken boullion, sherry, salt, and mushrooms, cooking for one more minute. Pour over crusts.

4 portions

OYSTERS ROQUEFORT

Creamy and succulent.

> *24 medium oysters, in the half shell*
> *1 1/2 ounces Roquefort cheese, at room temperature*
> *6 tablespoons butter, at room temperature*
> *6 green onions, minced*
> *2 garlic cloves, pressed*
> *1 large tomato, chopped*
> *1/4 cup fresh parsley, minced*

Combine Roquefort, butter, green onion, garlic, and blend well. Set aside.

In a medium saucepan, parboil oysters in a small amount of water for about 3 minutes, or until plump. Drain and return oysters to the half shell. Set shells on a baking sheet spread with a layer of rock salt. The rock salt will balance the shells. Top the oysters with the Roquefort mixture, then with tomatoes and parsley.

Broil in the oven for about 8 minutes, until Roquefort mixture is melted and bubbly. Serve immediately.

4-6 portions

OYSTERS ON THE ROCK

One of our experiments that turned out to be a great success.

> *24 medium oysters, in the half shell*
> *1 bunch fresh spinach, stemmed*
> *1/2 cup butter, melted*
> *1 tablespoon Ouzo*
> *1 1/2 cups Parmesan cheese, grated*

Blanch spinach for 30 seconds in boiling water. Drain and set aside.

In a medium saucepan, parboil oysters in a small amount of water for about 3 minutes, or until plump. Drain and return oysters to their shells. Set shells on a baking sheet spread with a layer of rock salt. Top each oyster with a dollop of spinach.

In a small saucepan, melt butter and Ouzo together. Drizzle this mixture over oysters, and top with grated Parmesan cheese. Broil in the oven for about 5 minutes, until the cheese is bubbly and hot.

4-6 portions

GRILLED OYSTERS

This brings out the best in an oyster, and in a beach party. I usually count on four to six oysters per person.

36 oysters in the shell
Melted butter or herb butter

Wash oyster shells thoroughly. Place oysters, with cupped side of shell down, on a grill about 4 inches from hot coals. Roast for 10-15 minutes or until shells begin to open. Serve in the shells with melted butter.

ISLAND OYSTER BAKE

The anchovies are a subtle enhancement.

18 large oysters, in the half shell
1/4 cup butter
1 1/2 tablespoons all-purpose flour
1 cup whipping cream
2 anchovy fillets, rinsed, drained, and minced
Grated rind of one lemon
Freshly ground white pepper
3/4 cup diced Monterey Jack, Havarti, or Muenster cheese

Garnish:
Minced parsley
Lemon wedges

Preheat oven to 375 degrees.

In a medium saucepan, parboil oysters in a small amount of water for about 3 minutes or until plump. Drain and return oysters to the half shells. Set oyster shells on a baking sheet spread with a layer of rock salt. The rock salt will balance the shells. Set aside.

Melt butter in a 1-quart saucepan. Over low heat, stir in flour with a wire whisk to form a smooth paste. Remove from heat and gradually stir in cream until smooth. Return to medium heat, and cook, stirring constantly, until thickened. Blend in minced anchovies and lemon rind. Add pepper to taste.

Pour white sauce over each oyster in the shell and top with a few cubes of cheese. Bake for 10 minutes. Sprinkle with fresh parsley and garnish with lemon wedges.

4 portions

SCALLOPS

The pink scallops swim rhythmically to the movement of the sea, a beautiful sea sight with a sweet taste. I prefer these steamed, like little-neck clams, and served in their lacy shells with drawn butter. Or add their special color to your bouillabaise.

The purple-hinged rock scallop is a diver's treasure, found below the, low tide line in rocky terrain, attached to rocks, sharing their shells with barnacles.

The rock scallop is non-commercial and a rarity.

The bay scallop is smaller, about half an inch across, and commonly available at the fish market. Their sweet, nutty flavor is a delicacy.

BAY SCALLOPS AND ASPARAGUS

Accompany with a nice Vouvray.

1 bunch fresh asparagus
1/2 cup butter
1 onion, sliced thin
1 clove garlic, pressed
1 pound bay scallops
1 tablespoon Dry Wit sherry
1/2 cup seasoned bread crumbs
1/4 cup Parmesan cheese, grated
3 tablespoons parsley, chopped

Garnish: Lemon wedges

Steam asparagus until tender-crisp.

Meanwhile, melt butter in a medium skillet. Add onions and garlic and saute until onions are limp. Add scallops and sherry. Saute for about 3 minutes, until scallops just turn opaque.

On individual ovenproof serving plates, arrange asparagus in rows. With a slotted spoon, distribute the scallop mixture along the center of the asparagus rows. Sprinkle bread crumbs, Parmesan, and parsley on top of scallops. Drizzle drippings from scallop mixture on top. Place under broiler until lightly browned.

Serve with lemon wedges.

4 portions

SCALLOP QUICHE

A tasty seafood luncheon with sauteed shrimp and a Washington Chenin Blanc.

1 9-inch pastry shell
2 tablespoons butter
1/4 cup minced onion
1 tablespoon tomato paste
1/4 cup Marsala wine
3/4 pound scallops, cut into 1/2-inch pieces
2 tablespoons minced parsley
2 tablespoons minced chives
Freshly ground pepper
1 1/4 cups grated Gruyere cheese
1 cup whipping cream
1/2 cup half-and-half
4 large eggs, lightly beaten
1 large egg yolk
1/2 teaspoon basil
1/4 teaspoon fennel seeds
Dash of cayenne pepper

Preheat oven to 400 degrees and bake pastry shell for 8-10 minutes in a quiche or pie pan.

Lower oven to 375 degrees.

Melt butter in a small skillet. Add onion and saute until soft. Stir in tomato paste. Add wine and cook over high heat for 1-2 minutes, until sauce is reduced to 2 tablespoons. Stir in scallops, parsley, and chives. Cook for about 1 minute. Season with pepper. Spoon mixture into pastry shell and sprinkle with cheese.

In a bowl, combine cream, half-and-half, eggs and egg yolk, basil, fennel seeds, and cayenne. Pour over cheese in pastry shell.

Bake for 35-40 minutes until set in center. Cool on rack for about 10 minutes before serving.

6-8 portions

SCALLOPS WITH SHALLOT AND BASIL SAUCE

Serve in big scallop shells and enjoy with a French white burgundy.

1 pound scallops
1 tablespoon lemon juice
1 tablespoon olive oil
2 tablespoons butter
3 tablespoons chopped shallots
2 cloves garlic, pressed
2 tablespoons white wine
1 tablespoon chopped fresh basil
Salt
White pepper

Garnish: 1 tablespoon chopped chives

Sprinkle scallops with lemon juice. Season with white pepper. Melt 1 tablespoon of butter and olive oil in a medium skillet, and saute shallots for 1 minute. Add scallops and saute for about 3 minutes, until they just turn opaque. Add garlic, wine, basil, and remaining butter, and stir to blend with drippings. Season with salt and white pepper.

Spoon into serving dishes and garnish with chives.

4 portions

SCALLOP AND WATER CHESTNUT KEBABS

Start a summer barbecue here.

6 12-inch bamboo skewers

1/2 pound thinly sliced bacon
6 ounces bay scallops
8 ounces water chestnuts, whole
1/3 cup soy sauce
2 tablespoons rice wine vinegar
1 1/2 tablespoons sugar
1 tablespoon Chinese rice wine
2 garlic cloves, pressed
1 teaspoon minced fresh ginger

Partially cook bacon until it is light brown, yet still limp. Cut each slice in half.

Weave bacon strips between scallops and water chestnuts on skewers. Arrange in a shallow dish. Combine remaining ingredients in a food processor or blender and mix well. Pour over kebabs, cover, and refrigerate for 3 hours, turning frequently.

Prepare fire, allowing coals to burn down to a moderate temperature. Set grill about 4 inches above coals. Drain marinade from kebabs. Grill kebabs until scallops are barely firm, about 4-6 minutes per side.

6 portions

ABALONE

Ah, abalone. Sport harvesting of the northern abalone brings this marvelous mollusk with its pearly interior and sweet rich meat fresh to our supper table.

Here at the fish markets the abalone is from Alaska waters. If you are using fresh abalone, pound the muscle with a meat mallet to tenderize. If you are using fresh frozen abalone, the freezing process actually breaks down the fibers and less tenderizing is needed.

I prefer this delicacy of the sea lightly sauteed in butter and topped with fresh lemons.

ABALONE WITH FRESH LEMONS

This sweet, nutty delicacy makes a festive entree with a crisp, colorful garden salad and a loaf of warm sourdough bread. This is a very rich dish, so portions may be small.

1/2 cup butter
1 large Walla Walla sweet onion, sliced
2 fresh lemons, sliced
1/4 cup white wine
4-6 whole abalone, cut into steaks and lightly pounded
Freshly ground pepper

Garnish:
Fresh parsley sprigs
Fresh lemon slices

Melt butter in a large heavy skillet. Add onions and cook until limp. Add lemon slices. Add wine and bring to a simmer. Add prepared abalone and quickly saute. The meat will turn an opaque color and be very tender. Be careful not to overcook, for this will make the abalone tough.

Season with freshly ground pepper, garnish with parsley and lemon slices, and serve immediately.

4-6 portions

ABALONE CORDON BLEU

For an elegant dinner, add Cold Cucumber-Mint Soup, a fresh garden salad, fluffy rice, and good wine.

4 large abalone
8 thin slices of cooked turkey
8 thick slices of Swiss or Monterey Jack cheese
3 eggs, beaten
2 cups seasoned cracker crumbs
Safflower oil
8 slices of pineapple

PINEAPPLE SAUCE

$^1/_2$ cup pineapple juice
$^1/_2$ cup champagne or white wine

Slice each abalone into four steaks and tenderize with meat mallet. Preheat oven to 400 degrees.

Layer a slice of abalone, a slice of turkey, and a slice of cheese. Top with another slice of abalone. Secure with toothpicks. Repeat procedure until eight layered abalone sandwiches are made.

Dip each abalone sandwich into beaten eggs, then into cracker crumbs.

Heat safflower oil in a large skillet. Add abalone sandwiches in batches and saute until golden brown. Transfer to a large baking dish, top each sandwich with a slice of pineapple, and bake in the oven for 8 minutes.

While abalone is baking, combine pineapple juice and champagne or wine in a small saucepan and bring to a boil.

Serve immediately with warm pineapple sauce. Make sure to either remove all toothpicks or warn your guests of their presence.

8 portions

SEAFOOD IN SHELLS

Scallops and shrimp presented in their own special plates—sea shells. This may be served as a first course or as a luncheon with a fresh garden salad.

6 4-inch scallop shells
2 tablespoons butter
2 green onions, minced
1/4 pound whitefish, boned and cut into small pieces
1/4 pound sea scallops
1/4 pound small shrimp, shelled and deveined
2 tablespoons chopped fresh parsley
Freshly ground white pepper
Salt
1 cup white sauce
2 tablespoons fine dry breadcrumbs
2 tablespoons freshly grated Parmesan cheese

Preheat oven to 350 degrees.

Melt butter in a large skillet over medium heat. Saute green onion until soft. Add fish, scallops, and shrimp and simmer gently until scallops and shrimp just start to turn opaque and fish just starts to flake when tested with a fork. Remove from heat.

Gently stir in parsley. Add salt and pepper to taste. Fold in white sauce. Divide mixture among scallop shells, and sprinkle with bread crumbs and Parmesan cheese. Place on baking sheet and bake until lightly browned and bubbly, about 10-15 minutes.

WHITE SAUCE

3 tablespoons butter
2 1/2 tablespoons all-purpose flour
1 1/2 cups hot milk
Salt
Freshly ground white pepper

Melt butter in a saucepan over medium low heat. Gradually stir in flour and whisk quickly to produce a smooth roux. Cook for 3-5 minutes. Remove the pan from the heat and gradually add hot milk. Return to heat, stirring constantly until sauce thickens. Season to taste with salt and pepper. Remove saucepan from heat and place a piece of waxed paper directly on top of the sauce to prevent a crust. Set aside until ready to use.

6 portions

BEER-BOILED SHRIMP

Shell these spicy shrimp at the table with bowls of cocktail sauce for dipping and a big salad and French bread on the side.

> *3 pounds unshelled shrimp ($^1/_2$ pound per person)*
> *6 cups beer*
> *2 tablespoons vinegar*
> *2 tablespoons salt*
> *2 bay leaves*
> *1 teaspoon mixed pickling spices*
> *3 ribs celery*
> *1 small onion, quartered*
> *2 tablespoons red pepper flakes*

Pour beer, vinegar, and salt into a large saucepan. Wrap bay leaves, pickling spices, celery, onion, and red pepper flakes in a cheesecloth square and tie at top. Place in saucepan with liquid and bring to a boil.

Add unshelled shrimp. Return water to a simmer and cook until shrimp turn pink, about 1-4 minutes. Drain immediately and serve hot. Supply small bowls for shells.

6 portions

SAUTEED SHRIMP

Delightfully simple.

> *Olive oil*
> *Fresh garlic, minced*
> *Salt*
> *Shrimp, raw in the shell*
> *Fresh lemon*

In a heavy skillet, heat olive oil and garlic. When garlic begins to brown, add about a fourth as much shrimp as the pan will hold. Add some salt. Toss the shrimp until the shells are bright red. Squeeze half of the lemon over the shrimp and toss in the pan several more times.

Enjoy.

PAELLA

Invite the neighbors over for this all-embracing Spanish classic.

1 chicken piece per serving
2 onions, chopped
1/3 cup olive oil
2 1/2 cups long grain rice
4 1/2 cups chicken stock
1/2 teaspoon saffron
1 green pepper
1 red pepper
4 cloves garlic
1 pound garlic sausage, browned
1 pound small shrimp
1 cup peas

Garnish:
1 cup black olives
Cherry tomatoes, seeded and peeled

Preheat oven to 375 degrees. Roast chicken pieces until done. Set aside and keep warm.

Saute onion in olive oil in a large saucepan. Add rice and saute until rice turns opaque. Add chicken stock and saffron. Cover and simmer gently for 20 minutes, stirring once or twice.

Chop peppers into 1/2-inch pieces. Press garlic. Slice sausage into 1/2-inch pieces. Add to rice and stir well. Cook for 5 minutes more. Stir in shrimp and peas.

Arrange chicken pieces on top of rice mixture in a large flat baking dish, and pour chicken juice over all. Bake for 10 minutes and serve at once. Garnish with olives and tomatoes.

6-8 portions

STEAMED MUSSELS

When you walk along a beach, look for the bluish-black mussels that cluster among the rocks. At low tide, pick the mussels, wash and scrub the shells, and scrape off their beards. These blue mussels are also available at the market. I allow between 12 and 20 mussels per person. Supply plenty of good crusty bread for dipping in the broth.

4 pounds washed mussels
1/4 cup butter
6 shallots or green onions (white part only)
2 cloves garlic
1 cup dry white wine
1/4 cup minced parsley
1 bay leaf
Freshly ground pepper
Melted butter for dipping mussels

In a large kettle, saute shallots and garlic in butter until soft. Add wine, parsley, bay leaf, and pepper. Bring to a boil. Add mussels, cover, and simmer gently just until shells open, about 4-6 minutes. Discard any mussels that do not open. Spoon mussels and broth into individual serving dishes.

Supply bowls of melted butter for dipping.

BUTTER CLAMS

Butter clams are large, hard-shelled, grayish-white clams whose shells are marked by concentric rings. They live on sand-gravel beaches, below the low tideline. To harvest, one needs a bucket, a small shovel, an eye for their oval holes, and a picnic to complete the outing.

We harvest during low tide for a few days, counting our limits, then clean the clams and can their sweet meat for delicious chowders when the tides are high.

Butter clams are tender and sweet, either lightly breaded and quickly fried as clam strips or simply sauteed and served with fresh lemon wedges.

When buying butter clams, look for very fresh ones. If the shells are partially open and do not respond to a touch and close, they should not be eaten.

CANNING BUTTER CLAMS

Clean clams from their shells, cut out their stomachs, and rinse well. Chop and pack into sterile pint canning jars to within 1 inch of the top. Fill jars with clam juice and a small amount of hot water, if needed – also to within 1 inch of the top. Adjust hot, sterile lids. In a pressure canner, process for 90 minutes at 10 pounds of pressure with the appropriate amount of water for capacity of canner. (See instructions supplied with canner).

LITTLENECK CLAMS

Littleneck clams are smaller than butter clams and are commonly called steamers. Their shells have concentric rings with ridges radiating from the hinges. Two species of littleneck clams live along our beaches: native littlenecks and Japanese littlenecks, also known as Manila clams. The Manilas were introduced by accident with oyster seed from Japan, and they became quite prolific here.

Dig for littlenecks during a minus tide with a small shovel, rake, or empty oyster shell. They are found close to the gravel surface. Enjoy your Department of Fisheries limit and respect the clams' beach homes by filling in your holes and thus not burying them under shovelfuls of gravel or mud.

Scrub the clams in a tidepool or under running water to remove sand from the shells. Place them in a bucket of fresh seawater and allow them to stand for 24 hours in a cool, shady place. They will filter themselves clean of sand.

STEAMED LITTLENECKS

I think littlenecks are best simply steamed and served in their shells with melted butter. To steam, place the clams in a steamer or large kettle with 1/2 inch of fresh water or dry white wine. Cover tightly and steam for about 10 minutes, or until the shells partially open. Discard clams that do not open.

Put clams into large bowls and serve hot with plain melted butter, or add some garlic and herbs from your garden.

Let the broth settle, and then gently pour it into mugs and sip a delicious clam nectar. I always try and save some of the nectar for a chowder or bouillabaisse.

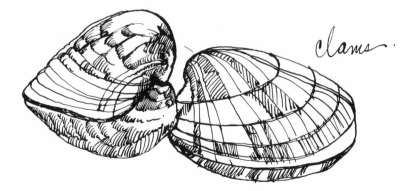

clams

FRESH CRACKED DUNGENESS CRAB

For supper by the sea.

Over an open-pit fire, bring a large kettle of sea water to a rolling boil. If sea water is not available, add 1 part salt to 16 parts regular water. Put a live crab in boiling water upside down. Cover and boil for 20 minutes. Remove from boiling water and quickly cool in cold water, keeping the shell upside down.

When cool, discard the top shell, yellow fat/butter, and gills. Flush the cavity with cold running water.

Crack the shell and taste the sweet flavor.

CRAB QUICHE

Serve with a Chenin Blanc or a Northwest Riesling. I bake this quiche in a clay pie plate—it makes an unrivaled flaky crust. For a change from crab, this recipe is also delicious with canned salmon.

> 1 unbaked 9-inch pie shell
> 1 tablespoon butter
> 1 small onion, chopped
> 4 eggs, slightly beaten
> 2 cups light cream
> 1/2 teaspoon salt
> Freshly ground pepper
> Dash of cayenne
> 1 1/2 cups crab meat
> 1/4 pound Gruyere cheese, shredded

Preheat oven to 425 degrees.

Line your unbaked pastry shell with waxed paper and fill half full with raw macaroni or dried beans. Bake for 7 minutes. Remove from oven and remove waxed paper and macaroni or beans. Reduce oven heat to 400 degrees.

Saute onion in butter. In a mixing bowl, combine eggs, cream, salt, pepper, and cayenne. Add sauteed onions.

Pat crab meat dry. Scatter crab and cheese in pastry shell. Pour in egg mixture. Bake for 35-40 minutes, until the center is set. Remove from oven and cool for 5 minutes before serving.

6 portions

SHELLED CRAB AU GRATIN

For dinner guests, serve in sea shells for a first course, or in a casserole with crackers as an appetizer.

$^1/_2$ *cup butter*
1 large onion, chopped
1 bunch green onions, chopped
2 hard-boiled eggs, mashed
4 cups crab meat
1 cup half-and-half
$^1/_2$ *cup minced fresh parsley*
6 cloves garlic, minced
1 teaspoon salt
$^1/_2$ *teaspoon freshly ground pepper*
Hot pepper sauce
1 cup seasoned bread crumbs
4 tablespoons sherry
8 teaspoons fresh lemon juice
Butter

Preheat oven to 400 degrees.

Melt butter in a large skillet over medium heat. Add onions and cook until soft. Remove from heat and add eggs, crab, half-and-half, parsley, garlic, salt, pepper, pepper sauce, and half the breadcrumbs. Stir well. Return to heat and cook for about 5 minutes. Remove from heat and stir in sherry.

Place in a shallow casserole or divide mixture into individual ramekins or baking scallop shells. Adjust seasoning. Sprinkle with remaining breadcrumbs and lemon juice. Top each serving with a pat of butter. Bake until tops are golden brown. Serve hot or cold.

8 portions

Butcher
BLOCK

Palace Meat Market
Mount Vernon — 1910.

ROASTED ORANGE DUCK

Two of the early entrepreneurs on Samish Island set up a business supplying boxes of picked and dressed wild ducks to fancy Seattle restaurants. Although no one of my acquaintance has had the experience of the two young men who bagged 150 ducks during a casual afternoon hunt in 1910, we are still blessed with an abundance of waterfowl wintering on our bays and inlets. Surround your plump trophy with mounds of wild rice and usher in the colors of autumn.

> 1 medium to large duck
> 1 apple, quartered
> 1 tablespoon butter
> 1/4 cup honey
> 1/4 cup orange juice
> 1 teaspoon orange peel
> 1/2-inch piece fresh ginger root, chopped,
> 1 teaspoon fresh basil, or 1/4 teaspoon dried

Preheat oven to 325 degrees.

Wash and dry duck well. Rub inside cavity with salt, and stuff apple quarters inside.

In a small saucepan over low heat, heat butter, honey, orange juice, orange peel, ginger, and basil until the butter is melted.

Place a large piece of foil in a shallow roasting pan and place the duck in the center of the foil. Pour half of the butter mixture into its cavity. Pour the remainder over the outside. Double seal the duck inside the foil.

Roast for 1 hour and 45 minutes. Open the foil and brown for 10-15 minutes longer. Remove apples and discard. Slice duck and pour liquid over slices to serve.

4 portions

BLUEBERRY DUCK BREASTS

When the berry season is upon you, be sure and put away a bottle of delicious vinegar and some frozen blueberries for this hunting season special.

4 duck breasts, skinned, boned, and split in half
Salt
Freshly ground pepper
1 cup light rose wine
4 tablespoons raspberry-blueberry vinegar
1 tablespoon fresh tarragon

Immerse Romertopf clay cooker in water and soak for 10 to 15 minutes. Drain.

Pat duck breasts dry and rub with salt and pepper.

Combine wine, vinegar, and tarragon and pour over the duck breasts in the clay cooker. Place in a cold oven, set the temperature at 400 degrees, and bake for 45-60 minutes.

If you do not have a clay baker, preheat the oven to 375 degrees. Place the duck in a shallow baking dish, cover with vinegar mixture, and seal tightly with foil.

When duck is done, remove from oven and serve on a warm platter topped with Blueberry Sauce.

RASPBERRY-BLUEBERRY VINEGAR

1/4 cup raspberries
1/4 cup blueberries
1 1/2 cups light red wine vinegar

Crush berries through a food mill or chop coarsely in food processor. Transfer to a bowl and blend in vinegar. Cover and let stand for several days in the refrigerator. Strain and bottle. Keep refrigerated.

BLUEBERRY SAUCE

3/4 cup orange juice or chicken stock
2 tablespoons currant jelly
1 teaspoon cornstarch
1/2 cups frozen blueberries, rinsed and thawed

In a saucepan over medium heat, combine orange juice or stock and jelly. Dissolve cornstarch in a small amount of water and add to saucepan. Blend well and bring to a boil. Add blueberries and stir until the mixture is slightly thickened, about 5 minutes.

4 portions

SMOTHERED DUCK

Take a deep breath and enjoy this lavish fall dish.

1 duck, cut into serving pieces
1 teaspoon salt
1/4 teaspoon freshly ground pepper
1 teaspoon fresh thyme, or 1/2 teaspoon dried
1/2 cup all-purpose flour
1/2 cup vegetable oil
1 cup half-and-half
1 small onion, sliced

Preheat oven to 325 degrees.

Mix together salt, pepper, thyme, and flour. Dredge duck pieces in mixture.

Heat oil in a heavy skillet and fry duck pieces over medium heat for about 30 minutes, until well browned on both sides. Add half-and-half and onion slices to pan, cover, and bake for one hour.

3-4 portions

CHICKEN SALTIMBOCCA

Enjoy with steamed fresh broccoli, a Soave wine, and dinner guests.

¹/₃ cup fine dry bread crumbs
2 tablespoons grated Parmesan cheese
2 tablespoons fresh parsley, minced
3 whole large chicken breasts, skinned, boned, and halved
6 thin slices of boiled ham
6 slices of mozzarella cheese
1 medium tomato, seeded and chopped
1 teaspoon sage, crushed
4 tablespoons butter, melted

Preheat oven to 350 degrees.

Combine breadcrumbs, Parmesan cheese, and parsley in a bowl, and set aside.

Place chicken breasts boned side up on a cutting board. Place a piece of clear plastic wrap over the chicken. Pound lightly with a meat mallet, working from the center out to shape breasts in an approximate 5-inch square. Remove wrap.

Place a piece of ham and a slice of mozzarella cheese on each cutlet. Top with some tomato and sage. Tuck in sides and roll up cutlets jelly-roll style, pressing to seal well.

Dip chicken rolls in melted butter, then roll in seasoned bread crumb mixture. Place in a shallow baking dish, and bake for 30-40 minutes.

4-6 servings

SPICED CHICKEN STRIPS

Serve with Sesame Broccoli.

3 pounds chicken breasts, boned and skinned
1 medium onion, chopped
1 head garlic, peeled
5 tablespoons peanut oil
1/4 cup red wine vinegar
3 tablespoons catsup
2 tablespoons fennel
2 tablespoons cumin
2 tablespoons paprika
20 peppercorns
1-inch piece fresh ginger root, peeled and chopped
Seeds from 8 pods of cardamom
8 whole cloves
2 teaspoons cilantro
2 teaspoons salt
1 teaspoon cinnamon
1/4 teaspoon ground red pepper

Cut chicken breasts into 1 1/2 or 2-inch strips.

Combine rest of ingredients in blender and process until well mixed. Place chicken strips in a large bowl. Add marinade and stir to coat. Cover and chill for 4-6 hours.

Broil marinated chicken for about 2 minutes on each side.

Serve on platter surrounded by Sesame Broccoli.

6 portions

RASPBERRY CHICKEN

Accompany this glamorous dish with wild rice and great green vegetables. Bring the raspberries back in the dessert. I bake this recipe in a Romertopf terra cotta clay baker. Immersed in water before each use, the unglazed clay absorbs the water, which is then released during cooking, blending with the natural juices of whatever is inside. This self-basting beauty enhances full flavors and tender foods such as choice chickens, duck and lamb, corn on the cob, and potatoes. After many suppers, my pot has succulently seasoned.

> *3 or 4-pound chicken, whole*
> *10 small yellow onions, whole or quartered*
> *4 tablespoons raspberry vinegar*
> *2 cups chopped fresh tomatoes with juices*
>
> *Option: If using a roaster, add 3 cups chicken stock*

If using a Romertopf, prepare clay baker by immersing in water for 10-15 minutes. Drain.

Place chicken in clay baker. Stuff 4-5 onions inside chicken, and place the remaining around the sides. Pour raspberry vinegar over chicken. Layer chopped tomatoes over top.

Cover pot and place in center of cold oven. Set oven to 400 degrees and bake for 1½ to 2 hours.

If you do not have a clay baker, preheat the oven to 375 degrees and bake the chicken in a covered roasting pan with 3 cups of chicken stock.

4 portions

FRESH HERB CHICKEN

An afternoon walk through Lavonne's garden is a delight to the senses, as one sees, smells, and smothers in the fifty-five herbs growing there. My garden grows fewer herbs, yet favorites. And then there are those in the kitchen cupboard that I have dried. When a recipe calls for a fresh herb that I don't have, or a dried herb that I have fresh, I have a formula that I've worked out over the years: I use 2 or 3 fresh portions to equal 1 dry portion.

> *3 whole chicken breasts, skinned and halved*
> *6 tablespoons olive oil*
> *6 tablespoons fresh chives, tarragon or other herbs, chopped*
> *³/4 cup fresh lemon juice*
> *6 tablespoons fresh parsley, chopped*

Prepare Romertopf by immersing in water for 10-15 minutes. Drain. Place chicken pieces in clay baker. Rub olive oil over chicken, top with fresh herbs and parsley, and pour lemon juice over all. Cover pot and place in center of cold oven. Set oven at 450 degrees and bake for 40-60 minutes.

If you do not have a clay cooker, preheat the oven to 375 degrees, wrap the chicken in double foil, and bake for about 40 minutes.

4 portions

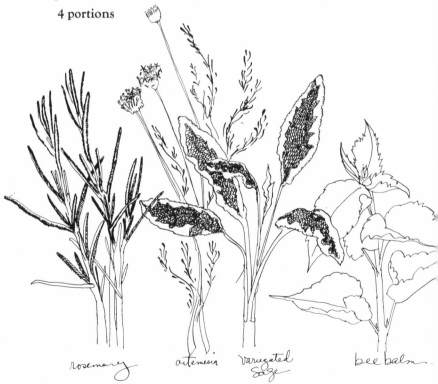

rosemary   artemesia   variegated   bee balm
                                sage

COUNTRY FRIED CHICKEN

I love this country farm meal served with warm onion cornbread and garden fresh vegetables.

> *3-pound chicken, cut into serving pieces*
> *2 cups milk*
> *1-2 cloves garlic, pressed*
> *2 cups all-purpose flour*
> *1 teaspoon freshly ground pepper*
> *Salt*
> *1 teaspoon sage*
> *1/4 cup butter*
> *1/4 cup oil*

In a medium bowl, combine chicken, milk, and garlic. Soak for 3-4 hours or overnight in refrigerator. Drain and pat dry.

Preheat oven to 350 degrees.

In a separate bowl, combine flour, pepper, salt, and sage. Dredge chicken in flour mixture.

In a heavy skillet, melt butter and oil. Brown chicken pieces on all sides, then drain skillet of all but a small amount of drippings. Return chicken to skillet and place in oven. Bake for 45-60 minutes. Check after 30 minutes, and cover if chicken is starting to get too dark.

4-6 portions

SAUSAGE-STUFFED LEG OF LAMB

This roast young lamb is full of seasonings and perfect for an Easter feast.

5-6 pound leg of lamb, trimmed and boned
3 tablespoons butter, softened
2-3 large cloves garlic, crushed or pressed
1 teaspoon salt
3/4 teaspoon freshly ground pepper
1 tablespoon crushed rosemary

STUFFING

3/4 pound lean ground pork
3 green onions, sliced
1 egg, lightly beaten
1/2 cup chopped fresh parsley
1 tablespoon finely shredded orange peel
3/4 teaspoon ground cumin
1/2 teaspoon freshly ground pepper
Salt

Garnish: Fresh mint leaves

To make stuffing, combine ground pork, green onions, egg, parsley, orange peel, cumin, ground pepper, and salt. Mix well, cover, and refrigerate until ready to use.

Preheat oven to 450 degrees.

Set butterflied lamb skin side down on working surface. Pound to flatten slightly. Mix butter, garlic, salt and pepper to form a paste. Rub half of the mixture thoroughly into the lamb. Spread with stuffing and reshape leg. Sew closed with kitchen string; tie crosswise at 1-inch intervals and twice around the length to hold stuffing. Rub outside of lamb with remaining butter mixture, then rub with rosemary. Set on rack in roasting pan and roast for 20 minutes. Reduce oven temperature to 350 degrees and roast an additional 1 hour, or until meat thermometer reads 135 degrees.

Transfer to a heated serving platter and garnish with mint. Let stand for several minutes before slicing.

6-8 portions

SPINACH-STUFFED LAMB

Dave and Dolly Hickox provide us with high-quality choice cuts of local meats along with good, old-fashioned service across their counter at Warren's Meats in Burlington. They suggested this recipe for a special dinner.

> *5-6 pound leg of lamb, boned and butterflied*
> *2 tablespoons butter*
> *2 tablespoons olive oil*
> *1/2 cup chopped shallots*
> *3 cloves garlic, crushed*
> *5 bunches fresh spinach, chopped*
> *1/4 cup brandy*
> *1/4 cup tomato paste*
> *1/4 cup fresh basil*
> *2 teaspoons fresh rosemary*
> *2 teaspoons fresh thyme*
> *1/4 cup ricotta cheese*
> *1 1/2 cups ground sausage*
> *Salt*
> *Freshly ground pepper*

Preheat oven to 425 degrees.

Melt butter and olive oil in a large frying pan. Add shallots and garlic and saute over medium heat for 3 minutes. Add spinach and continue cooking for 2 minutes, until spinach is just wilted. Remove from heat and set aside.

In a separate pan, mix brandy, tomato paste, basil, rosemary, and thyme. Cook over medium heat until thickened. Let cool, and add the ricotta cheese and ground sausage. Press juice from spinach mixture and add to cheese and sausage.

Place lamb skin side down on flat surface. Spread stuffing mixture along center of leg, and roll lamb around it. Tie together with kitchen twine.

Place in open pan and cook in oven at 425 degrees for 30 minutes. Reduce heat to 350 degrees and cook for another 1 1/2 hours, until internal temperature reaches 135 degrees. Do not overcook.

6-8 portions

MUSTARD CHOPS

Pick up nice lamb chops at the market and you'll have an elegant entree for guests within moments.

> *12 lamb chops, 1 inch thick*
> *1 cup Dijon mustard*
> *3 tablespoons soy sauce*
> *1-2 cloves mashed garlic*
> *1 tablespoon chopped fresh rosemary, savory, or thyme*
> *1 tablespoon chopped fresh parsley*
> *1 teaspoon grated ginger or ¹/₂ teaspoon dry*
> *3 tablespoons olive oil*

Blend mustard, soy sauce, garlic, and herbs with a whisk. Beat in olive oil drop by drop until the mixture looks like thick cream. Spread the mustard mixture on the lamb chops and let them sit at room temperature for an hour or so.

Preheat oven to 375 degrees.

Put chops on rack in pan and roast for 30 minutes. Broil for 2-3 minutes to brown tops before serving.

6-8 portions

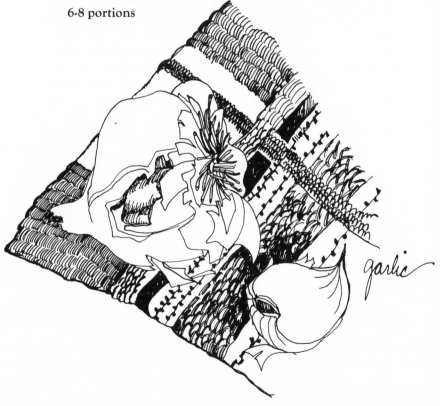

garlic

BARBECUED LAMB CHOPS

These chops soak overnight in a marinade spiced with nutmeg and cloves. They're wonderful with baked potatoes and stuffed tomatoes.

12 lamb chops, 1 inch thick
2 cloves garlic, split
2 teaspoons salt
Freshly ground black pepper
1 teaspoon crumbled dried rosemary leaves
2-3 cardamom seeds
$1/4$ teaspoon nutmeg
$1/2$ teaspoon cloves
$1/2$ cup finely chopped onion
2 tablespoons lemon juice
$1/4$ cup red wine vinegar
$2/3$ cup olive oil

Blend garlic in mortar with salt, pepper, rosemary, cardamom, nutmeg, and cloves. Combine with onion, lemon juice, vinegar, and olive oil.

Place lamb chops in shallow glass dish and pour marinade over. Cover and refrigerate overnight, turning once.

When ready to cook, drain and save marinade. Place lamb on grill 8-10 inches from medium-hot coals. Grill, basting with marinade, until well-browned on one side, from 5-10 minutes. Do not cook too fast. Turn and grill another 5-10 minutes to brown the other side. Test with a sharp knife—meat should be juicy and pink, and feel firm when pressed. Serve immediately.

6 portions

DOLMATHES

Prepare your own fresh leaves or buy them in a jar—either way, these stuffed grape leaves are a splendid and exotic treat.

1/4 cup olive oil
1 medium onion, finely chopped
1 pound lean ground lamb
1/2 cup short-grain rice
1/4 cup chopped fresh dill or 1 tablespoon dried dillweed
1/4 cup chopped fresh mint
1/3 cup pine nuts
1/4 cup water
2 tablespoons tomato paste
Freshly ground pepper
Salt (if fresh leaves are used)

4 dozen prepared fresh grape leaves OR 1-quart jar grape leaves in brine, well rinsed
3/4 cup rich chicken broth
3 tablespoons fresh lemon juice

Garnish: 1 lemon, thinly sliced

Heat oil in a large skillet. Add onion and saute until translucent. Add ground lamb, stirring to break into pieces. Add rice, dill, mint, pine nuts, water, and tomato paste. Season to taste with pepper and salt, if necessary. Cook over medium heat until water is absorbed, about 10 minutes.

Cover bottom of Dutch oven with a layer of grape leaves. Stuff remaining leaves by placing leaf, shiny side down, on a smooth surface. Put a spoonful of meat mixture in the center of each leaf. Fold base over stuffing, then fold sides of leaf over, tucking edges in snugly. Roll up and tuck tip of leaf beneath to prevent unrolling. Arrange tip side down in Dutch oven.

Add broth to within 1 inch of top layer. Use any leftover leaves to cover top layer. Place plate upside down over top layer and press with a heavy object. Cover and bring to a boil over medium heat. Reduce heat and simmer until rice is tender, about 45 minutes. Sprinkle with lemon juice and cook for 5 minutes longer.

Let cool to room temperature or chill thoroughly. Serve garnished with lemon slices. Dolmathes can be prepared 2-3 days before serving and refrigerated.

4-5 dozen dolmathes

TO PREPARE FRESH GRAPE LEAVES

Use the tender leaves of wild or cultivated grapevines. Pick the choice ones by counting down from the tip of a vine and selecting the third and fourth leaves. Snip stems from leaves, pile in stacks of a dozen, and drop each stack into boiling water, pressing leaves down for a few seconds until they are pliable. Lift out, drain, and cool. Leaves may be dampened slightly and stored for a few days in a plastic bag, then used to make dolmathes.

EGGPLANT MOUSSAKA

The glossy purple skins wrap a marvelous moussaka mold.

3 large eggplants
Salt
1 cup olive oil
1 large onion, chopped
2 tablespoons olive oil
1 pound lean ground lamb or beef
2 cloves garlic, minced
2 cups fresh tomatoes, chopped
3 tablespoons tomato sauce
2 tablespoons fresh marjoram
Salt
Freshly ground pepper
¹/₂ cup dry bread crumbs

SAUCE

1¹/₂ tablespoons butter
2 tablespoons flour
1 cup warm milk
¹/₄ teaspoon salt
2 eggs, beaten
²/₃ cup ricotta cheese

Remove green caps from eggplants and quarter lengthwise. Sprinkle cut surfaces with salt and let stand for 20 minutes; pat dry. Heat oil in a large skillet and brown the cut sides of eggplant. Drain on paper towels. Scoop out flesh with a spoon, leaving skins intact. Chop flesh and set aside.

Saute onion in oil in a hot skillet. Add lamb or beef and garlic and cook for 20 minutes, until brown. Add tomatoes, tomato sauce, reserved eggplant flesh, marjoram, salt, and pepper. Cook until liquid has all evaporated, and set aside to cool. Add bread crumbs and mix well.

Preheat oven to 350 degrees.

To make sauce, melt butter in a medium saucepan. Whisk in flour and stir until smooth. Slowly stir in milk. Add salt and continue cooking, stirring constantly, until sauce is thickened and smooth. Remove from heat. Whisk eggs into sauce, add cheese, and mix well. Pour sauce into meat mixture and blend well.

Oil a 3-quart charlotte mold or other deep dish and arrange eggplant shells vertically around the edges, purple sides against the mold. Overlap sides of eggplant slices and let pointed ends meet at the center of the bottom of the mold. The sides and bottom should all be neatly covered.

Spoon filling into the mold, and fold eggplant skins over the top. Cover mold with foil and a lid, and set in a pan of boiling water which is deep enough that water reaches about halfway up the sides of the mold. Bake for 1 1/2 hours.

Remove from oven and hot water bath and let cool for 1 hour. Invert onto a serving platter, cut into wedges, and garnish with large slices of fresh tomato.

10 portions

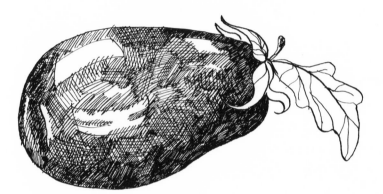

KEFTETHES

Spicy Greek meatballs topped with a dilly yogurt sauce.

1 pound ground lamb
1 cup finely chopped onion
2 cloves garlic, minced
1/2 cup finely chopped parsley
1 tablespoon chopped fresh mint or 1 1/2 teaspoons dried
1 egg
2 tablespoons olive oil
2 tablespoons fresh oregano or 2 teaspoons dried
1 teaspoon salt
Dash pepper
2 slices of white bread, crusts removed
1/2 cup dry red wine
Flour
1 tablespoon olive oil
2 tablespoons butter

Combine lamb, onion, garlic, parsley, mint, egg, oil, oregano, salt, and pepper in a large mixing bowl.

In a small bowl, moisten bread with wine; add to meat mixture and mix thoroughly. Shape mixture into balls 2 inches in diameter; dust with flour.

Heat oil and butter in a medium skillet; brown meatballs on all sides. Keep warm in a covered casserole until ready to serve. Top with yogurt sauce.

YOGURT SAUCE

1 cup plain yogurt
4 medium cloves garlic, minced
2 tablespoons fresh lemon juice
5 tablespoons olive oil
1 tablespoon fresh dill or 1 1/2 teaspoons dried
Salt
Pepper

Process all ingredients in food processor or blender until well-mixed. Pour into a jar, cover, and refrigerate until ready to use.

4 portions

ROASTED PERFECTION

Dolly Hickox says that this is the way to ensure a perfect roast every time. It tastes best when allowed to marinate for two days before cooking.

> *3-4 pound prime rib roast*
> *$^1/_2$ cup lemon juice*
> *4 cloves garlic, crushed*
> *3 tablespoons fresh herbs, minced*

Place roast in a plastic bag with lemon juice, garlic, and herbs. Marinate overnight or longer in the refrigerator, then let it sit at room temperature for an hour or so before cooking.

Preheat oven to 500 degrees.

Place roast in an uncovered roasting pan and place in oven. DO NOT OPEN OVEN DOOR UNTIL ROAST IS DONE. Cook at 500 degrees for 30 minutes. Turn oven off and let the roast cook for 20 more minutes per pound, but do not open the oven door. This method produces a perfect medium-rare roast.

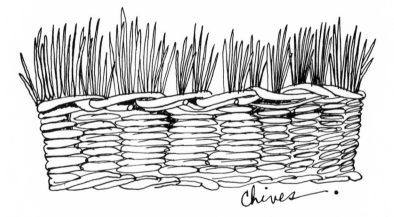

Chives

MARINATED GRILLED FLANK STEAK

Choose a good dry red wine for the marinade, then serve the rest of the bottle with the steak.

1 ¹/₂ pounds flank steak, trimmed

MARINADE

Juice of 1 lemon
¹/₂ cup soy sauce
¹/₄ cup dry red wine
3 tablespoons olive oil
2 tablespoons Worcestershire sauce
3 tablespoons honey
1 large clove garlic, sliced
¹/₂ inch fresh ginger, sliced

Mix all marinade ingredients in a pan or dish which is just big enough to hold the flank steak. Marinate the flank steak, turning occasionally, for 2 to 12 hours in the refrigerator.

Broil meat over hot coals for 5 minutes per side for rare meat. Slice the meat on the diagonal across the grain and serve.

3-4 portions

STEAK WITH TOMATO AND CAPERS

Unbeatable.

> *Flank, loin, or T-bone steaks to serve 4*
> *2 tablespoons olive oil*
> *¹/₂ cup minced onion*
> *1 clove garlic, pressed*
> *6 tomatoes, quartered*
> *2 teaspoons basil*
> *1 teaspoon oregano*
> *¹/₄ cup oil-cured black olives*
> *2 tablespoons capers, drained*
> *Salt*
> *Freshly ground pepper*

Panbroil steaks in a heavy skillet in olive oil and set aside, keeping warm. Add onion to the skillet in which the steaks were cooked and saute over medium heat för 2 minutes. Stir in garlic and cook 1 minute longer. Add tomatoes and their juice, basil and oregano, and simmer for 5 minutes, stirring frequently. Stir in olives and capers and season with salt and pepper. Pour over steaks. Serve immediately on warm plates.

4 portions

FIERY RIBS

Everyone needs a house barbecue recipe. Here's one that works for ribs and burgers alike.

Enough ribs to serve your crowd (about 1 pound/person)
Brown sugar
Barbecue Sauce

Place ribs in boiling water to cover and continue to boil for 30-45 minutes.

Preheat oven to 350 degrees.

Drain water and roll ribs in brown sugar while still hot. Place in a baking dish and cover with barbecue sauce. Bake for 1 hour or grill over hot coals.

BARBECUE SAUCE

2 large onions, finely chopped
1 tablespoon garlic, finely chopped
3 tablespoons vegetable oil
1-pound can crushed tomatoes
12-ounce can tomato puree
1/4 cup coarsely chopped fresh hot chilies or crushed hot dried chilies
2 tablespoons dry mustard
2 tablespoons sugar
1 tablespoon distilled light vinegar
1 1/2 teaspoons salt

Saute onion and garlic in vegetable oil until soft. Stir in remaining ingredients. Bring to a boil over high heat. Cook briskly until thick, stirring occasionally, for 30-45 minutes. This sauce is best prepared a day in advance, and it can be stored up to a month in the refrigerator.

TOM'S TACOS

The raisins were introduced by Tom and add a sweetness to the common taco.

>1 pound lean hamburger
>1/2 cup raisins
>1 medium onion, chopped
>1 medium green pepper, chopped
>1 garlic clove, minced
>2 cups salsa
>1/4 cup water
>
>1 dozen flour tortillas
>1 pound Cheddar cheese, shredded
>1 small head iceburg lettuce, shredded
>2 large tomatoes, diced
>1 cup black olives, sliced
>
>Garnish:
>1 cup sour cream
>Salsa

In a large skillet, brown hamburger and drain off any excess fat. Add raisins, onion, green pepper, garlic, salsa, and water and simmer until onion and green peppers are tender and sauce is reduced to a thick-filling consistency.

In a medium skillet, lightly fry tortillas in a small amount of oil, or heat on a dry, hot skillet over medium heat, for about 30-60 seconds per side, so that the tortillas are still soft and pliable.

Fill each tortilla with taco meat, and top with cheese, lettuce, tomatoes, and olives. Serve with bowls of sour cream and salsa.

6 portions

CHORIZO

Serve this Mexican sausage for breakfast with fluffy scrambled eggs and warm flour tortillas, or feature it in tacos and enchiladas. Make sure the ground pork you use has some fat in it—this will make the lean meat tender and keep it from becoming hard and stiff when cooked. The vinegar and spices are the preservatives for this sausage, and it keeps for quite a long time if refrigerated or frozen. The longer it keeps, the better it tastes.

> *5 pounds ground pork, at room temperature*
> *$^2/_3$ cup vinegar*
> *3 teaspoons salt*
> *6 teaspoons cumin seeds, ground (fresh, if available)*
> *12 cloves garlic, ground*
> *4 red poblano chilies*
> *$^1/_2$ package chili seasoning mix*

Mix pork and vinegar together. Place in a cheesecloth bag or a colander covered with foil and drain in a warm place for 12 hours.

Grind red poblano chilies and soak in boiling water for 10-15 minutes. Mix with the remaining ingredients and mix well with pork.

Refrigerate overnight. This sausage can either be wrapped in foil just as it is and used as bulk sausage, or it can be stuffed into casings and made into links. Links need to soak in water for two hours. Both types of sausage freeze beautifully. If frozen, allow mixture to stand 1 day to thaw.

SWEDISH MEAT BALLS

Accompany with red potatoes and tender carrots from your garden. Make them "fancy" sometimes with a cream sauce.

> *1 pound lean ground beef*
> *1 pound pork sausage*
> *$1^1/_2$ teaspoons ground ginger*
> *Freshly ground pepper*
> *6 cups water or beef stock*

Mix all ingredients well. Form into very small balls, and place them on a plate as you go. Slide the whole amount into 6 cups of salted boiling water or beef stock. Cook for about 10 minutes and test for doneness.

4-6 portions

BREAD
Winners

Huntoon Building
Anacortes 1905.

CRACKED WHEAT BREAD

Enjoy the aroma of baking bread and the rich texture of cracked wheat spread with fresh sweet butter. This is a favorite.

> *1 cup cracked wheat or bulghur*
> *2 cups water*
> *2 packages active dry yeast*
> *$^1/_2$ cup warm water*
> *$^1/_2$ cup molasses*
> *1 tablespoon salt*
> *2 cups cold milk*
> *4 tablespoons shortening*
> *up to 12 cups unbleached white flour*
>
> *Option: substitute 1 cup wheat germ for 1 cup white flour*

Put cracked wheat and 2 cups of water in a saucepan and bring to a boil. Cover and turn off heat. Let stand for 10 minutes.

Sprinkle dry yeast over $^1/_2$ cup of warm water.

In a large bowl, combine molasses and salt. Add cracked wheat, then cold milk, then yeast and shortening. Gradually add flour. Knead until smooth and elastic. Shape dough into a ball and place in bowl. Cover bowl with towel and let rise in a warm place until the dough doubles, about 1 $^1/_2$ - 2 hours.

Punch down the dough, divide it into thirds, and shape into loaves. Place into three greased loaf pans and let rise for another hour.

Preheat oven to 375 degrees.

Bake loaves for 45 minutes to one hour, until loaves are brown and sound hollow when thumped on the bottom. Remove loaves from oven and cool on a rack.

3 loaves

PAULINE'S BREAD

This sweet rye bread could be yours, too.

> 2 tablespoons active dry yeast
> 3 cups warm water
> 1/2 cup brown sugar
> 1/3 cup molasses
> 1 tablespoon salt
> 3 tablespoons melted shortening
> 1 1/4 cups rye flour
> 7-8 cups unbleached all-purpose flour

Dissolve yeast in warm water. Add brown sugar, molasses, salt, and melted shortening. Mix well. Add rye flour and 3 cups of white flour. Mix on electric mixer for 7 minutes. Work 4 more cups of flour in by hand.

Place dough in bowl and let rise in warm place until double, about 1-1 1/2 hours. Punch down, place in 2 greased loaf pans and let rise 1/2 to 1 hour more.

Preheat oven to 325 degrees. Bake on middle rack of oven for 35 to 50 minutes, until well browned. Remove from oven and cool on a rack.

2 loaves

HONEY WHEAT BREAD

This bread from The Calico Cupboard in LaConner won Best of Show
from the Wheat Growers of Washington.

4 cups lukewarm water
4 packages active dry yeast
7/8 cup honey
4 eggs
7/8 cup safflower oil
1 tablespoon salt
4 pounds wholewheat bread flour
1/4 cup gluten flour
3/4 cup powdered milk

Dissolve yeast in lukewarm water in a large mixing bowl. Add honey
and stir. Let the mixture stand for about 10 minutes to proof the yeast.
Blend in eggs, oil, and salt. With the dough hook on an electric mixer, or
by hand, add wholewheat flour, gluten flour, and powdered milk. Knead
for 10 minutes, until the dough cleans the bowl and is soft and elastic to
the touch. Place dough in oiled bowl, turn upside down to oil top, and
cover with plastic wrap or a damp cloth. Let rise in a warm place until
double in bulk, about 1½ hours.

When the dough has doubled, turn onto an oiled surface and pound
it down. Let it rest for 2-3 minutes. Divide into 4 pieces. Knead each
piece for 2-3 minutes. Shape into loaves and place in oiled loaf pans.

Preheat oven to 375 degrees.

Let loaves rise in pans until nearly double in bulk. Bake for approximately 40 minutes, or until loaves are golden brown and sound hollow
when tapped. Brush with butter and cool on wire rack.

4 loaves

WHEAT BUNDLES

This recipe makes two small round loaves, perfect for Sunday's stew.

2 packages active dry yeast
2 tablespoons firmly packed brown sugar
1 teaspoon salt
4 cups all-purpose flour
1 cup whole wheat flour
2 cups milk
1/4 cup butter
1 egg
1 cup wheat germ

In a large bowl, combine sugar, salt, yeast, and 2 cups of flour.

Heat milk and butter until very warm (115 degrees) and stir into flour mixture. Add egg, 1 cup of wheat flour, and the wheat germ. Beat until well blended. Mix in about 1 1/2 cups more flour to make a stiff dough.

Turn dough out onto floured board and knead until smooth – about 10 minutes – adding more flour as required to prevent sticking. Divide dough into 2 equal pieces and shape into smooth balls. Place on a greased baking sheet. Cover and let rise in a warm place until doubled, about 30 minutes.

Preheat oven to 375 degrees.

Bake until browned (15-20 minutes). Serve hot or cold.

2 small round loaves, about 6 portions.

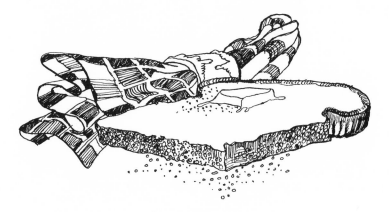

SWEDISH LIMPA BREAD

1 ³/4 cups boiling water
¹/4 cup firmly packed brown sugar
¹/4 cup butter
¹/4 cup dark molasses
1 tablespoon salt
¹/4 cup caraway seeds
¹/4 cup warm water
1 package active dry yeast
3 cups unbleached all-purpose flour
3 cups rye flour
1 egg white

Combine boiling water, brown sugar, butter, molasses, salt, and caraway seeds in a large bowl and let stand until lukewarm. Stir yeast into ¹/4 cup of warm water and add to mixture in bowl. Add 2¹/2 cups unbleached flour and beat until smooth. Blend in rye flour, and then add enough of the additional unbleached flour to form a soft dough. Turn onto a lightly floured board and cover with bowl. Let rest for about 10 minutes.

Knead dough until smooth and elastic. Place in a greased bowl, turning to coat all sides. Cover with plastic wrap and a warm, damp towel and place in a warm spot. Let rise until doubled in bulk.

Punch dough down and let rise again for 30 minutes. Punch down again, divide in half, and shape into loaves. Place in greased loaf pans, cover with plastic wrap, and let rise until doubled.

Preheat oven to 375 degrees.

Beat egg white lightly and brush over loaves. Bake for about 40-45 minutes, until loaves are well-browned and sound hollow when tapped. Remove from oven and cool on wire rack.

2 loaves

ONION CORNBREAD

Great with fried chicken and the in-laws.

>   *¹/₄ cup butter*
>   *2 medium onions, chopped*
>   *1 cup sour cream*
>   *¹/₄ teaspoon salt*
>   *1 cup shredded sharp Cheddar cheese*
>   *1 package (10 or 12 ounces) corn muffin mix*
>   *1 egg*
>   *¹/₂ cup milk*
>   *8¹/₂-ounce can creamed corn*
>   *3 drops red pepper sauce*

Preheat oven to 425 degrees.

Grease an 8-inch square pan and set aside.

Melt butter in a skillet over medium heat. Add onions and saute until tender, about 10 minutes. Cool slightly. Add sour cream, salt, and ¹/₂ cup Cheddar cheese. Set aside.

In a mixing bowl, combine corn muffin mix, egg, milk, corn, and hot pepper sauce. Stir until smooth. Spread batter into greased pan. Spoon onion mixture evenly atop the batter. Sprinkle with remaining ¹/₂ cup Cheddar cheese.

Bake for 30 to 35 minutes, or until a toothpick inserted in the center comes out clean. Serve warm.

9 portions

CHEESEY BREAD

Stop at the Washington Cheese Company in Mount Vernon and watch them make the cheese...then carry some home for this cheesey bread.

>   *1 loaf of French bread*
>   *¹/₂ cup butter*
>   *1 cup mayonnaise*
>   *1 cup shredded Cheddar or Monterey Jack cheese*
>   *Parmesan cheese, grated*
>   *Oregano*

Preheat oven to 300 degrees.

Melt butter, and stir in mayonnaise and cheese. Mix well. Cut bread into two halves lengthwise, and spread mixture over each side. Sprinkle with Parmesan cheese and oregano. Place on baking sheet, and bake until top begins to brown, about 5-8 minutes.

HARDANGER LEFSE

Every part of Norway has its own way of making lefse. A sweeter variety than the potato lefse, this recipe is shared by Ruth Bakke. Serve with a meal or just with coffee.

> 2 cups buttermilk
> 2 eggs
> $1/3$ cup sugar
> 1 teaspoon salt
> 1 teaspoon soda
> $1/4$ cup butter, melted
> 4-5 cups all-purpose flour
> $1/2$ cup melted butter
> $1/2$ cup sugar
> 1 teaspoon cinnamon

Mix buttermilk, eggs, sugar, salt, soda, and melted butter together. Add flour a little at a time. Cool dough.

Pinch off an egg-shaped piece of dough, and roll it out on a floured surface into a thin circle. Pick up lefse using a wooden dowel made for the purpose (available in Scandinavian stores) or by wrapping the dough around a rolling pin.

Shake off excess flour and lay dough circle on a lefse iron or flat griddle. Cook, turning once, until light brown on both sides. Cool and store dry if desired.

When ready to serve, sprinkle or dip lefse in cool water. Lefse will absorb water and soon be ready to serve. Stack lefse on a plate, placing paper towels between each piece. Let rest for 20 minutes.

Spread butter on each lefse, and sprinkle with cinnamon and sugar. Fold each lefse in half and cut into 2-inch diamond shapes. Serve or freeze for later use.

Lefse may also be served crisp by heating through in a slow oven.

SOPHIE JOHNSON'S POTATO LEFSE

My neighbor Wanda Peterson taught me how to make this delicious flat-bread. Spread with butter and eaten warm, lefse turns a Norwegian meal into a celebration.

4 cups potatoes, riced and chilled
1 cup all-purpose flour
1/4 cup oil
1 tablespoon sugar
1 teaspoon salt or less

The night before, boil, peel, and rice potatoes.

The next day, combine all ingredients in a large mixing bowl. Mix well. Form dough into 3/4-inch balls. On a covered and floured board, roll out dough very thin with a lefse rolling pin. Transfer to lefse griddle or cast iron frying pan. Cook, turning once, until lightly browned in spots. Remove from griddle and place on a clean towel to cool.

Spread with creamed butter. Sprinkle with sugar. Fold in the sides to make the circle a square, then fold the square in half. Slice into 1-inch wide pieces.

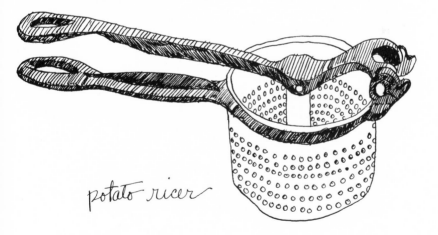

potato ricer

FLOUR TORTILLAS

Anita Guillen, a delightful Mexican woman, taught us to make these flour tortillas. They are well worth the handwork. The basic staple of the Mexican table, Anita calls them "our spoon and fork." Serve them plain with butter, or fill with chilies, eggs, or shredded cheese.

4 cups unbleached all-purpose flour
2 teaspoons baking powder
1 teaspoon salt
4 tablespoons shortening
1 cup plus 2 tablespoons water

Mix flour, baking powder, and salt in a large mixing bowl. With hands, work in shortening, until it is incorporated with the flour. Add water to form a soft dough and knead for about 4 minutes. Separate dough into about 14 small balls and roll out into thin circles on a lightly floured board.

Heat a cast iron skillet or griddle over medium-high heat. Cook each tortilla until it is light brown on the underside and bubbles appear on the surface, about 20 seconds. Turn and cook the other side for another 20 seconds.

Keep warm in a cloth-lined basket, and serve hot. Do not cover with foil or plastic, for these will cause the tortillas to sweat and become soggy.

1 dozen tortillas

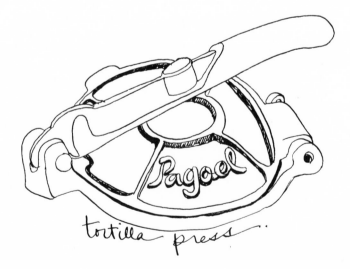

tortilla press

Prize
PIES

EUROPA TART

A favorite from Cafe Europa, a lovely custard tart topped with the first strawberries of spring and followed by ripe fruits and berries all summer long. This recipe makes two generous tarts. The custard stores well in the refrigerator, so keep the extra dough frozen and you'll be set for the berry season.

TART DOUGH

1 cup butter
1 cup sugar
1 beaten egg
1/2 teaspoon vanilla flavoring
2 1/2 cups flour
Ground almonds (optional)

Preheat oven to 350 degrees.

Cream butter and sugar. Add egg and vanilla and beat well. Gradually add flour until absorbed but not sticky. Refrigerate and roll out for one or two 11-inch tart pans. Prick shells, and sprinkle on the ground almonds for crispier texture if desired. Bake until golden, about 15 to 20 minutes. Remove from oven and cool on wire rack.

CUSTARD BUTTERCREAM FILLING

1/2 cup butter
1/2 cup cream cheese
1 cup confectioners' sugar
Vanilla flavoring

1/2 cup cornstarch
1 cup sugar
4 cups milk
2 egg yolks
2 teaspoons vanilla
1 cup whipped cream

Cream butter and cream cheese together. Add confectioners' sugar a little at a time, beating well after each addition. Beat mixture until light and fluffy. Add vanilla to taste. Set aside.

In a large saucepan, mix cornstarch, sugar, and milk and whisk to remove lumps. Cook over medium heat until thickened, stirring constantly, or place in microwave on high for 13 minutes, stirring frequently if microwave doesn't rotate food.

Remove from heat and beat thoroughly with a wire whip. Beat in egg yolks. Cook for 2-3 more minutes until thickened. Add vanilla flavoring and butter/cream cheese mixture and blend well. Place in refrigerator and cool quickly. Fold in whipped cream.

FRUIT TOPPING

2 cups fresh fruit or berries
1 cup red currant jelly
1 tablespoon water

Clean berries or fruit and slice if necessary.
Heat currant jelly with water in a small saucepan. Remove from heat and allow to cool.

TO ASSEMBLE TART

Spoon cooled custard filling into baked tart shell. Arrange whole or sliced berries or fruit on top of custard. Brush cool glaze on top of berries or fruit and refrigerate until ready to serve. Top with dollops of whipped cream.

Two 11-inch tarts

BLACKBERRY COBBLER

The valley is full of berries. Himalayan blackberries are the most plenti-
ful; tiny seedless wild ones are the most delectable. This old-fashioned
cobbler does justice to both.

1 1/2 cups sugar
1/2 cup unbleached white flour
1 teaspoon salt
8 cups blackberries
3 tablespoons lemon juice
3 tablespoons butter

BISCUIT TOPPING

2 cups sifted unbleached flour
4 teaspoons baking powder
3 tablespoons sugar
1 teaspoon salt
1/2 cup butter
2/3 cup milk
1 egg, slightly beaten

Preheat oven to 400 degrees.

Mix together sugar, flour, salt, berries, and lemon juice. Pour into a
13 X 9-inch baking dish, and dot with butter. Bake for 15 minutes, until
hot and bubbly.

Meanwhile, make biscuit topping. Mix together sifted flour, baking
powder, sugar, and salt in a mixing bowl. Cut in butter until mixture
resembles coarse cornmeal. Add milk and beaten egg, and stir with a
fork just until blended.

When blackberry mixture is hot and bubbly, spoon biscuit mixture
on top in 10 or 12 dollops. Return to oven for 20 minutes, until biscuits
are browned. Allow to cool for at least 10 minutes before serving. Top
with ice cream or whipped cream.

12 portions

LEMON-BLUEBERRY TART

Tangy lemon custard topped with fresh sweet blueberries: a fabulous summer treat.

1 9-inch pastry shell, baked

LEMON CUSTARD

10 tablespoons sugar
4 egg yolks, room temperature
6 tablespoons fresh lemon juice
1/4 cup unsalted butter, cut into pieces
pinch of salt
2 teaspoons finely shredded lemon peel

In a heavy non-aluminum saucepan, beat sugar and yolks until well blended. Add lemon juice, butter, and salt. Stir with a wooden spoon over medium-low heat for about 8 minutes,until mixture thickly coats back of spoon; do not boil. Remove from heat and stir in lemon peel. Cool. Cover with plastic wrap directly on top of custard and refrigerate for at least 1 hour.

Spread custard into pastry shell and set aside.

BLUEBERRY TOPPING

1/3 cup sugar
1 tablespoon cornstarch
1/2 cup water
1 1/2 teaspoons fresh lemon juice
3 cups fresh blueberries

In a heavy medium saucepan, combine sugar and cornstarch. Mix in water and lemon juice. Stir over medium heat, and bring to a full rolling boil. Cook until mixture thickens and turns translucent. Remove from heat. Mix in blueberries. Spread berry mixture evenly on top of custard. Refrigerate 30 minutes before serving.

8 portions

BLUEBERRY CHIFFON PIE

This is a beautiful purple chiffon pie from Anderson Blueberry Farm.

1 9-inch pastry shell, baked

2 cups blueberries
1/2 cup sugar
3 tablespoons cornstarch
4 tablespoons cold water
2 egg whites
1 1/2 tablespoons sugar
Whipped, sweetened cream

Boil the berries, sugar, cornstarch, and water until thick, stirring constantly.

Beat two egg whites until stiff. Add 1 1/2 tablespoons sugar. Fold berry mixture into egg whites. Pour into baked shell and cover with whipped cream.

6 portions

RED RASPBERRY PIE

A stunning red pie stuffed with ripe whole raspberries.

1 9-inch baked pie shell

1 quart fresh raspberries
3/4 cup sugar
2 1/2 tablespoons cornstarch
1/4 teaspoon salt
1/2 cup water
1/2 cup fresh orange juice

Whipped cream

Remove 1 cup of raspberries and puree in blender or press through sieve. Set aside.

In a medium saucepan, combine sugar, cornstarch, salt, water, and orange juice. Cook over low heat, stirring constantly, until thickened, about 10 to 15 minutes. Add pureed raspberries.

Place whole raspberries in pie shell. Pour syrup over the berries. Chill in refrigerator for at least 4 hours.

Serve garnished with sweetened whipped cream.

GOOSEBERRY PIE

I'm glad there is a gooseberry bush in my garden, because this is my father's favorite pie.

4 cups gooseberries (about 2 pints), stemmed
1 1/2 - 2 cups sugar
1/4 cup cornstarch
1/2 teaspoon cinnamon
1/4 teaspoon salt

Pastry for a 2 crust, 9-inch pie
1 tablespoon butter

About 2 hours before serving or early in the day, preheat oven to 450 degrees.

If gooseberries are large, slice them in half.

In a medium bowl, combine sugar, cornstarch, cinnamon, and salt; add gooseberries and toss well. Set aside while preparing pastry.

Roll out half of pastry and line a 9-inch pie plate. Spoon gooseberry filling evenly into crust and dot with butter. Roll out top pastry crust, and center over filling in bottom crust. Trim pastry edges leaving a 1-inch overhang. Fold this overhang under on pie-plate rim and flute edges. Cut a few short slashes or a design in the center of top crust.

Bake for 10 minutes at 450 degrees, then turn oven temperature down to 350 degrees and bake for 1 hour or until pastry is golden. Serve warm or cold.

6 portions

gooseberries

WILD HUCKLEBERRY TART BLACK SWAN

This tart is designed for the tiny red huckleberries of the Skagit foothills. Other fruit can be used, but select fruit that is on the tart side, such as green apples or tart pears.

Pate brisee or other pastry dough

1 1/2 cups ricotta cheese
5 tablespoons sugar
1 teaspoon vanilla
1-2 cups fresh huckleberries
18-ounce jar currant or plum preserves
1/4 cup creme de cassis

Preheat oven to 400 degrees.

Roll out pastry dough on a lightly floured board. Butter a tart pan and fit dough into pan; cover with foil and fill with beans or rice to weigh down pastry while baking. Bake for 10 minutes, remove from oven, and cool completely.

In a food processor or blender, combine ricotta cheese, sugar, and vanilla. Process until very smooth and spread into cooled tart shell. Cover with a single layer of huckleberries.

Heat preserves and creme de cassis, and reduce until thick. Pour over huckleberries. Cool before serving.

PEACH PIE IN A COCONUT SHELL

COCONUT PIE SHELL

1 cup shredded coconut
$^1/_2$ cup wheat germ
1 tablespoon honey
1 tablespoon oil

Combine all ingredients and pat into a 9-inch pie pan. Chill thoroughly before filling.

FRESH PEACH FILLING

$^1/_2$ cup water
$^3/_4$ cup sugar
1 cup crushed peaches
3 tablespoons flour
1-2 tablespoons water
2 cups thin-sliced peaches

Whipping cream

Combine water and sugar in a medium saucepan and bring to a boil. Add crushed peaches. Mix flour and water together and add to liquid to thicken. Remove from heat and cool.

Fill pie shell with sliced peaches, and pour cooled mixture over top. Chill and top with whipped cream.

MRS. SUMMER'S RHUBARB CUSTARD PIE

1 9-inch pastry shell

4 cups diced rhubarb
1 1/2 cups sugar
3 egg yolks
1/2 cup flour
3 tablespoons milk
3/4 teaspoon nutmeg

Preheat oven to 400 degrees.
Place rhubarb in bottom of pie shell.
Combine sugar, egg yolks, flour, milk and nutmeg. Beat well and spread over rhubarb.
Bake at 400 degrees for 20 minutes. Lower heat and continue to bake at 350 degrees for 20 more minutes. Allow to cool, and add meringue.

MERINGUE

1 tablespoon cornstarch
1/2 cup boiling water
3 egg whites
6 tablespoons sugar
Pinch of salt

Dissolve cornstarch in just enough cold water to moisten. Add to boiling water and cook until thick and clear, stirring constantly. Remove from heat and set aside to cool.
Preheat oven to 375 degrees.
Beat egg whites until stiff. Add salt and sugar gradually. Beat in the thoroughly cooled cornstarch mixture until the egg whites gain the right consistency to stand in peaks. Pile on top of pie and brown in oven.

RHUBARB PIE

Refresh a summer afternoon with a slice of rhubarb pie, a glass of chilled rhubarb wine, and conversation with friends.

1 1/2 cups sugar
1/3 cup all-purpose flour
1 tablespoon grated orange peel
1/4 teaspoon salt
4 cups rhubarb, cut into 1-inch pieces (about 3 pounds)

Pastry for a 2-crust, 9-inch pie
2 tablespoons butter

Preheat oven to 425 degrees.

In a large bowl, combine sugar, flour, orange peel, and salt. Add rhubarb and toss well; set aside while preparing pastry.

Roll out half of pastry and line the bottom of a 9-inch pie plate. Spoon rhubarb mixture evenly into crust, and dot with butter.

Roll out top pastry crust and center over filling in bottom crust. Trim pastry edges, leaving a 1-inch overhang. Fold overhang under on pie plate rim and flute edges. Cut a few short slashes in center of crust.

Bake for 40-50 minutes until the crust is golden. Serve warm or cold.

6 portions

WALNUT TART

Celebrate fall with this beautiful brown tart, a recipe from Marie Paule Braule.

Pastry for 9-inch crust

1 1/3 cups walnuts
3/4 cup sugar
1/2 cup softened butter
2 large eggs
3 tablespoons espresso or very strong coffee
1/4 teaspoon salt

3/4 cup confectioners' sugar
3 tablespoons espresso
1 1/2 teaspoons vanilla extract
Walnut halves

In a food processor or blender, whirl walnuts and sugar. Add butter, eggs, coffee, and salt. Blend until smooth and refrigerate.

Preheat oven to 375 degrees.

Line a 9-inch removable bottom pie pan or springform pan with pastry, pour in walnut mixture, and bake for about 35 minutes.

Dissolve confectioners' sugar in espresso and vanilla. Pour over warm tart, and decorate with walnut halves.

GRANDMA KNUTZEN'S PUMPKIN PIE

A flourish for fall and the star of our family's Thanksgiving table.

3 unbaked pastry shells

5 eggs, well beaten
3 cups sugar
1 teaspoon salt
1 teaspoon nutmeg
1 teaspoon cinnamon
1 teaspoon ginger
4 cups pumpkin puree
2¹/₂ cups milk

Preheat oven to 450 degrees.

Combine eggs, sugar, salt, nutmeg, cinnamon, and ginger, mixing well. Add pumpkin, then milk. Mix thoroughly, and pour into pie shells. Bake at 450 degrees for 10 minutes. Reduce heat to 350 degrees and bake until a knife inserted in the center comes out clean.

3 pies

HONEY AND CHEESE PIE

A happy ending for a spicy Greek dinner.

> *1 9-inch pastry shell*
> *2 cups ricotta cheese*
> *³/4 cup honey*
> *3 medium eggs, lightly beaten*
> *1 teaspoon grated lemon peel*

Preheat oven to 350 degrees.

Line unbaked pastry shell with waxed paper and fill with dried beans. Bake for 10 or 15 minutes. Remove from oven, cool slightly, and remove paper and beans. Set aside to cool completely.

Combine cheese and honey in a mixing bowl. Add eggs and lemon peel and mix thoroughly. Pour filling into cooled crust and bake for about 1 hour, until top is golden brown. Serve at room temperature, topped with ripe berries or seasonal fruits.

6-8 portions

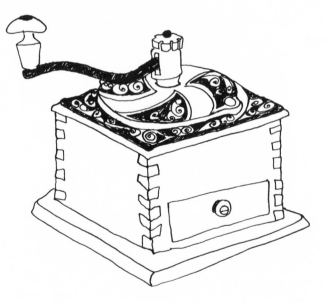

CHOCOLATE SILK PIE

A luxurious dessert from The Calico Cupboard in La Conner.

1 9-inch prebaked pie shell

3 ounces unsweetened chocolate
1 cup butter
1 1/2 cups sugar
1 1/2 teaspoons vanilla
4 eggs

Sweetened whipped cream
Grated chocolate curls

Melt chocolate in a double boiler over boiling water. Remove from heat and cool slightly. Cream butter. Gradually add sugar and blend in chocolate and vanilla. Add eggs one at a time, beating for 5 minutes between additions. Turn mixture into baked pie shell and chill for at least two hours.

Top with sweetened whipped cream and grated sweet chocolate curls.

SWEETENED WHIPPED CREAM

2 cups whipping cream
1/2 cup confectioners' sugar
3/4 teaspoon vanilla
1/2 teaspoon unflavored gelatin

Dissolve gelatin in 1 teaspoon of hot water and set aside. Beat whipping cream until it starts to thicken. Gradually add sugar, then vanilla and gelatin. Beat until stiff peaks form.

PASTRY CRUST

A good basic pie crust.

> *1 1/3 cups flour*
> *1/2 cup cold butter*
> *1 teaspoon salt*
> *1/4 cup cold water*

Cut together flour, salt, and butter into a coarse meal. Add water and work into dry ingredients to form a ball of dough. Handle lightly and quickly. Wrap dough in waxed paper and chill for about 90 minutes. On a lightly floured board, roll pastry out for desired shell.

One 10-inch crust

FLAKY PASTRY

Especially good for fruit pies or simple quiches. For a delightful nutty flavor, roll pastry dough out on whole wheat flour.

> *3 cups unbleached all-purpose flour*
> *1 1/2 cups vegetable shortening*
> *1 teaspoon salt*
> *1 egg*
> *1 tablespoon vinegar*
> *3-4 tablespoons water*

Cut shortening into flour and salt until mixture resembles coarse cornmeal. Beat egg, and add vinegar and water. Stir into flour-shortening mixture. Form a ball of dough, and wrap it in waxed paper. Chill. On a lightly floured board, roll dough out for desired shell.

Two 9-inch shells or one double crust.

PATE BRISEE

This pastry is ideal for custard fillings. Instead of rolling it out, you press it into the pie plate with your fingers.

> *2 cups flour*
> *Pinch of salt*
> *1 tablespoon sugar*
> *²/₃ cup butter*

Combine flour, salt, and sugar. Cut in butter with pastry blender or work in with your fingers until mixture is a coarse meal. Shape the dough into a ball, wrap, and chill for at least 45 minutes.

Preheat oven to 450 degrees for a prebaked crust.

Press pastry into a pie plate with your fingers until you have an even thickness and a smooth crust. Flute the edge. Line with wax paper, fill with dried beans, and bake for 10 minutes. Fill as desired and finish baking.

One 9-inch crust

PASTRY BRISEE

A perfect pastry for quiches.

> *1 ¹/₃ cups bleached all-purpose flour*
> *¹/₂ cup well-chilled salted butter, cut into small pieces*
> *¹/₂ teaspoon salt*
> *2 ¹/₂ tablespoons ice water*

Blend flour, butter, and salt with hands until the mixture reaches the consistency of coarse meal. Add water and blend with a fork until the dough gathers together. Gently form into a ball, and flatten into a disk. Cover with plastic wrap and refrigerate for at least 45 minutes.

Roll pastry out into a 12-inch round. Transfer to a 10-inch pie plate or tart pan. Fold the edges of pastry over to create a double thickness of dough around the rim. Flute or finish edges. Cover and refrigerate about 1 hour.

Preheat oven to 425 degrees.

Line pastry with foil, waxed paper, or parchment and fill with dried beans. Bake until firm, about 15 minutes. Remove parchment and beans. Pierce pastry all over with fork and bake for another 5 minutes, until pale golden brown. Cool on rack, and fill as desired.

One 10-inch crust

CAKE
Conclusions

Kransekake
Danish Wedding Cake

KRANSEKAGE

This Danish Wedding Cake is used throughout the Scandinavian countries by those who wish to preserve tradition, and it is almost always seen at the weddings of royalty. Tradition stipulates that a special bottle of wine be hidden in the center of the cake. When it is time to serve the cake, the top tiers are lifted off the very bottom one, leaving the wine exposed and ready to serve. The bottom ring is then broken into pieces and served, then the next largest ring is uncovered and broken, and so on until all the guests are served. The cake is crisp throughout, and the broken pieces are held in the hand and eaten as a cookie. To make a uniformly tiered cake, it is best to bake this in the special kransekage rings.

1 1/2 pounds almond paste
1 1/2 cups sugar
3 egg whites, slightly beaten
(1/2 egg white may be added so the dough is not too stiff)

Preheat oven to 325 degrees and grease kransekage rings well.

Mix ingredients thoroughly. Fill a large pastry bag which is equipped with either a plain or open star tube. Fill each ring. Keeping dough warm makes it easier to handle. Bake the rings only until surface is crusty and beginning to brown a bit. Do not allow them to take on a toasted appearance. Remove from rings as soon as they are cool enough to handle.

FROSTING

1 egg white
3-4 drops vinegar
Confectioners' sugar

Mix egg white and vinegar with enough confectioners' sugar to make a thin icing. With decorator and plain small tube, make drizzles and scallops on each ring. When icing is hard, tier rings according to size, placing a bit of icing here and there to keep rings from slipping. A top decoration may be added if desired. A few fresh flowers were placed in the top ring on my wedding day.

CARROT CAKE

This delicious moist cake is great at backyard picnics, or triple the recipe and tier it high for a wedding celebration. We did!

2 cups sugar
1 1/2 cups vegetable oil
4 eggs
2 cups unbleached all-purpose flour
1 teaspoon salt
2 teaspoons baking soda
2 teaspoons cinnamon
3 cups grated carrots
1/2 cup chopped nuts

Preheat oven to 350 degrees.

In a large bowl, mix sugar, oil, and eggs. Sift dry ingredients together, and gradually add to wet mixture. Stir in grated carrots and nuts. Pour into a greased and lightly floured 9 X 13-inch pan or 3 9-inch round layer cake pans.

Bake for 45 minutes. Remove from oven and cool on a wire rack. Frost with Cream Cheese Frosting.

CREAM CHEESE FROSTING

1 8-ounce package cream cheese, softened
3/4 cup butter, softened
1 pound confectioners' sugar
1/2 cup chopped nuts
2 teaspoons vanilla

Cream butter and cream cheese. Add confectioners' sugar and mix well. Add nuts and vanilla. Spread on cooled cake.

For frosting a wedding or anniversary cake, omit the nuts and spread the frosting smooth. Use a pastry bag with a simple tip to create borders around the cake, and decorate with fresh flowers. Simply beautiful.

ALICE'S APPLE CAKE

Tart Washington apples star in this hearty cake.

3 cups sifted all-purpose flour
1 teaspoon baking soda
1 teaspoon ground cinnamon
2 cups sugar
3 eggs
1¼ cups vegetable oil
1 teaspoon vanilla
¼ cup orange juice
1 tablespoon grated orange peel
2 cups grated unpared fresh apple
1 cup chopped walnuts
1 cup flaked coconut

Buttermilk sauce

Preheat oven to 325 degrees. Grease and flour a 10-inch tube pan.
Sift flour, baking soda, and cinnamon onto waxed paper.

Combine sugar, eggs, oil, vanilla, orange juice, and orange peel in a
large bowl. Beat with electric mixer until well blended. Stir in flour mixture until well mixed. Fold in apples, walnuts, and coconut.

Spoon into prepared tube pan. Bake in a slow oven for 1½ hours or
until top springs back when lightly pressed with fingertip. Cool in pan
on wire rack for 15 minutes.

Transfer cake from pan to a serving plate with a raised edge. Puncture
top of cake all over with a wooden pick or skewer. Spoon hot Buttermilk
Sauce over warm cake several times. Let stand for about an hour before
serving. Pour extra sauce into a small pitcher and serve with cake.

BUTTERMILK SAUCE

1 cup sugar
½ cup butter
½ teaspoon baking soda
½ cup buttermilk

Combine sugar, butter, soda, and buttermilk in a medium saucepan.
Cook over medium heat, stirring constantly, until mixture comes to a
boil. Remove from heat and spoon over cake.

APPLESAUCE CAKE

Mother says this is my father's favorite cake. Maybe it will be yours as well.

1 cup sugar
1/2 cup shortening
1 egg
1 3/4 cups sifted cake flour
1/2 teaspoon salt
1 teaspoon baking soda
1 teaspoon cinnamon
1 teaspoon cloves
1 cup raisins
1 cup nuts, chopped
1 cup thick, slightly sweetened applesauce

Preheat oven to 350 degrees.

Cream sugar and shortening. Add egg and beat well. Gradually blend in flour, salt, and soda. Add spices, raisins, and nuts; then stir in applesauce.

Bake in a 9 X 13-inch pan for 40 minutes. Frost with Caramel Icing.

CARAMEL ICING

1 cup brown sugar
3 tablespoons butter
3 tablespoons cream

Combine sugar, butter, and cream in a medium saucepan. Bring to a good rolling boil, then remove from heat. Beat until mixture reaches the consistency of frosting. If it gets too stiff, add a few drops of cream.

NUTTY BLUEBERRY CAKE

This lovely cake, studded with true blueberries and filberts, comes from Julie Pendergrast.

2 1/2 cups flour
1 teaspoon baking powder
1/2 teaspoon baking soda
1 cup butter cut into 16 pieces
1 1/4 cups sugar
1 teaspoon vanilla
1/2 teaspoon lemon rind
2 eggs
1 cup sour cream

BLUEBERRY FILLING

2 tablespoons sugar
2 tablespoons flour
1 1/2 cup blueberries
1/2 cup filberts, chopped medium-fine

TOPPING

1 1/2 tablespoons sugar
1/4 teaspoon cinnamon
Dash nutmeg

Preheat oven to 350 degrees. Grease and flour a 9-inch tube pan.
Stir together all filling ingredients and set aside.
Sift together flour, baking powder, and soda, and set aside.
In a large bowl, mix butter, sugar, vanilla, and lemon rind at medium speed. Beat in eggs, one at a time, until well blended. Beat in sour cream. At slow speed, gradually add flour mixture and mix well.
Turn about 1/3 of batter into prepared tube pan. Sprinkle with half the blueberry filling. Repeat layers. Spread with remaining batter.
Mix together sugar, cinnamon, and nutmeg for topping, and sprinkle over batter. Bake on rack below center of oven until done, about 55 minutes. Cool on a wire rack for 5 minutes, then loosen edges and turn onto rack to cool completely. Invert on a cake platter.

POPPY SEED CAKE

The poppy seeds flower in Lavonne Newell's big garden, the cake bakes beautifully in her kitchen, and her lavender borage flowers decorate the top.

3/4 cup butter
2 cups sugar
6 eggs
1/2 cup safflower oil
1 cup sour cream
3/4 cup cream sherry
1 small package instant vanilla pudding
3/4 cup poppy seeds
3 1/2 cups flour
1/2 teaspoon baking soda
2 1/2 teaspoons baking powder
1 teaspoon salt
1/2 teaspoon freshly grated nutmeg

Preheat oven to 350 degrees. Grease and flour an angel food tube pan and a loaf pan.

Cream together butter and sugar. Beat eggs and add to butter mixture. Add oil, sour cream, sherry, pudding mix, and poppy seeds and beat well.

Sift together flour, soda, baking powder, salt, and nutmeg. Beat into egg mixture and blend well. Pour batter into prepared pans and bake for 50 minutes to 1 hour.

ORANGE GLAZE

3 tablespoons melted butter
2 tablespoons milk
1 1/2 tablespoons freshly squeezed orange juice
1 1/2 teaspoons grated orange peel
2 cups confectioners' sugar

Melt butter together with milk, orange juice, and orange peel. Beat in confectioners' sugar, adding more if needed for thickening. Pour over cake.

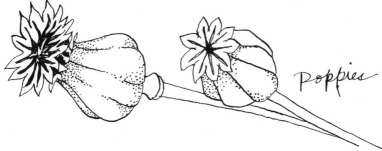

poppies

SPICY PRUNE CAKE

Linda's Grandma Beyler's recipe.

> *1 cup vegetable oil*
> *1 1/2 cups sugar*
> *3 eggs*
> *2 1/2 cups flour*
> *1 1/2 teaspoons salt*
> *1 teaspoon baking powder*
> *1 teaspoon baking soda*
> *1 teaspoon cinnamon*
> *1 teaspoon nutmeg*
> *1 teaspoon allspice*
> *1 cup prunes, chopped*
> *1 cup buttermilk*
> *1 cup nuts, chopped*

Preheat oven to 350 degrees. Lightly grease and flour a 13 X 9-inch pan.

In a large bowl, cream together oil and sugar. Add eggs one at a time, beating well after each addition. Sift together dry ingredients and add alternately to creamed mixture with prunes and buttermilk. Fold in nuts. Pour into prepared pan.

Bake for 35 minutes. Cool cake and frost with Caramel Glaze.

CARAMEL GLAZE

> *1 cup sugar*
> *1/2 cup buttermilk*
> *1/2 teaspoon baking soda*
> *1 tablespoon corn syrup*
> *1/2 cup butter*
> *1/2 teaspoon vanilla*

In a medium saucepan, combine the above ingredients. Over low heat, bring to a boil, stirring constantly. Boil for 10 minutes. Allow to cool before pouring over cake.

ITALIAN CREAM CAKE

Jolene Berry baked this festive cake for a birthday party among friends. It is now a favorite cake for celebrations of anniversaries, birthdays, and Sunday company.

> *5 eggs, separated*
> *¹/₂ cup butter*
> *¹/₂ cup shortening*
> *2 cups sugar*
> *2 cups cake flour*
> *1 teaspoon baking soda*
> *1 cup buttermilk*
> *1 teaspoon vanilla*
> *1 cup shredded coconut*
> *1 cup chopped pecans*

Preheat oven to 350 degrees. Grease and lightly flour 3 8-inch round cake pans.

Beat egg whites until stiff, and set aside.

Cream butter and shortening. Add sugar and beat well. Add egg yolks one at a time. Sift flour and soda together, and add to sugar and shortening mixture alternately with buttermilk. Blend in vanilla, then coconut and nuts. Fold in stiffly beaten egg whites.

Divide batter among 3 prepared pans and bake for 25 minutes. Cool on wire racks. Layer and frost with Cream Cheese Frosting.

CREAM CHEESE FROSTING

> *2 8-ounce packages cream cheese, softened*
> *¹/₄ cup butter, softened*
> *2 cups confectioners' sugar*
> *1 teaspoon vanilla*
> *¹/₂ cup chopped pecans*

Cream the cream cheese and butter together. Gradually add confectioners' sugar. Add vanilla, then nuts.

Spread frosting between each layer of cake and over top and sides.

DIVINE DECADENCE

A dense and dazzling chocolate-swathed filbert torte.

TORTE

7 eggs, separated
1 tablespoon white vinegar
1 tablespoon water
1 3/4 cups filberts, roasted and peeled
1 1/4 cups sugar
7 ounces semisweet chocolate
1 tablespoon baking powder
1/8 teaspoon salt
1/2 cup butter, at room temperature
1 tablespoon vanilla

Position rack in center of oven and preheat to 350 degrees. Butter two 9-inch round cake pans and line bottoms with parchment. Butter paper.

In a large bowl, beat egg whites until foamy. Add vinegar and water and continue beating until soft peaks form.

In a food processor or blender, combine nuts, sugar, chocolate, baking powder, and salt. Process until blended. Add butter and vanilla and process until well mixed. Add egg yolks one at a time and process until completely blended.

Spoon one third of egg whites on top of chocolate mixture and mix just until combined. Transfer this mixture into a bowl with remaining egg whites and gently fold until just combined. Divide batter between prepared pans. Bake for about 30 minutes, until toothpick inserted in center comes out clean.

Cool in pan for 10 minutes. Invert onto cooling racks. Remove paper and cool completely.

CHOCOLATE FILLING

2/3 cup whipping cream
1/2 cup butter
12 ounces semisweet chocolate
1 teaspoon vanilla
Pinch of salt

Bring cream and butter to a boil in a small heavy saucepan.

In a food processor or blender, finely mince the chocolate. With machine running, pour in hot cream mixture and blend until chocolate is melted. Add vanilla and salt and blend well. Transfer to bowl and cool completely.

TOPPING

1 1/2 cups well-chilled whipping cream
1 ounce semisweet chocolate
12-16 whole roasted filberts

TO ASSEMBLE TORTE

In a large bowl, whip cream until thick. Add 1/2 of the chocolate filling mixture and beat until fluffy.

Place one cake layer upside down on platter. Spread remaining chocolate filling over top of layer. Place 2nd layer right side up on top. Spread whipped cream and chocolate mixture over top and sides of torte, using a long thin spatula. With vegetable peeler, form curls of chocolate and sprinkle over top of cake. Place filberts around the top edge. Refrigerate cake for 3-5 hours, then let stand at room temperature for 1/2 hour before serving.

BOURBON FILBERT LOAF

A perfect holiday loaf and a welcome gift.

3 cups flour
1 cup sugar
4 teaspoons baking powder
1 1/2 teaspoons salt
1/4 cup butter
2 teaspoons grated orange rind
1 1/4 cups chopped filberts
1 egg
1 cup milk
1/2 cup bourbon

Preheat oven to 350 degrees. Grease and flour a 9 X 5 X 3-inch loaf pan.

In a large mixing bowl, combine flour, sugar, baking powder, and salt. Cut in butter until it resembles coarse crumbs. Add orange rind and filberts.

In a small bowl, combine egg, milk, and bourbon. Add liquid to dry ingredients, stirring just until blended. Turn into loaf pan and bake for 60-70 minutes. Remove from oven and sprinkle with 2-3 tablespoons more bourbon. Let cool in pan for 10 minutes. Turn onto rack and cool completely.

DATE CREME TORTE

A light and creamy torte, sweet with dates. Serve on dessert plates laced with doilies and accompany with a dessert wine. Luxury.

TORTE

¹/₃ cup all-purpose flour
1 tablespoon cornstarch
2 eggs, at room temperature
¹/₃ cup sugar
1¹/₂ tablespoons butter
1 teaspoon vanilla

Preheat oven to 325 degrees. Line a 9-inch round cake pan with parchment; butter and flour the paper.

Sift together flour and cornstarch. Set aside.

Whisk eggs and sugar together in a metal bowl or double boiler over simmering water until the mixture feels warm to the touch. Remove from heat. Beat with an electric mixer until ribbons form when beaters are lifted, about 8 minutes.

Add butter and vanilla, and gently fold in flour mixture. Pour into prepared pan. Bake until top springs back when lightly touched, about 20-25 minutes. Invert onto rack and cool completely.

FILLING

¹/₄ cup ricotta cheese
2 tablespoons sour cream
1 cup whipping cream
3 eggs, at room temperature, separated
¹/₂ cup sugar
1 cup milk, heated
2¹/₂ teaspoons unflavored gelatin
2 tablespoons cold water
1 teaspoon vanilla
¹/₂ teaspoon finely grated lemon peel
¹/₂ cup chopped dates
2 tablespoons fresh lemon juice

Whipped cream

Line a 9-inch round cake pan with plastic wrap.

In a small bowl, combine ricotta cheese and sour cream. Set aside.

In another small bowl, beat 1 cup of whipping cream until soft peaks form. Set aside.

In a heavy medium saucepan, whisk egg yolks and sugar together. Whisk in heated milk. Stir with a wooden spoon over medium heat until thick, about 8 minutes. Do not boil.

In a small bowl, sprinkle gelatin over cold water. Set in a pan of simmering water and stir until completely dissolved. Add vanilla and lemon peel, and blend into a custard. Set bowl in a pan of ice cubes and stir custard until cooled and slightly thickened.

Stir ricotta cheese mixture, whipped cream, dates, and lemon juice into custard. Pour into prepared pan, and top with cake. Refrigerate overnight. Invert onto serving platter, decorate with sweetened whipped cream, and serve.

TORTA DE ALMENDRA

An orange and almond flavored dream.

> 1 1/2 cups cake flour
> 1 cup sugar
> 1 1/2 teaspoons baking powder
> 1/2 teaspoon salt
> 3/4 cup milk
> 1/3 cup shortening
> 1 egg
> 2 teaspoons grated orange peel
> 1/4 cup sliced almonds
> 1 tablespoon sugar
> 2 tablespoons orange liqueur

Preheat oven to 350 degrees. Grease and flour a 9 × 1 1/2 " pan.

In a large mixing bowl, combine flour, 1 cup of sugar, baking powder, salt, milk, shortening, egg, and orange peel. Beat on an electric mixer at low speed for 30 seconds. Beat at high speed for 3 minutes. Pour into prepared pan and sprinkle with sliced almonds. Bake for about 40 minutes. Remove from oven and sprinkle with 1 tablespoon of sugar and drizzle with liqueur. Cool for 10 minutes before removing from the pan.

CHOCOLATE HAZELNUT TORTE

This scrumptious dessert is a specialty in the kitchen of the Cafe Europa. Serve with a full-bodied cup of coffee and listen to the faint moans of pure pleasure.

1 10-inch Chocolate Sponge
Hazelnut Liqueur Mixture
Hazelnut Filling
1 pint sweetened whipped cream
6 ounces semi-sweet chocolate, melted

Garnish: Sweetened whipped cream

CHOCOLATE SPONGE

6 eggs, at room temperature
³/₄ cup sugar
²/₃ cup unsifted flour
2 tablespoons cocoa
1 teaspoon baking powder
3 tablespoons melted butter

Preheat oven to 325 degrees.

Beat eggs with wire whip in mixer, gradually adding sugar until tripled in volume, about 5 minutes. Sift together flour, cocoa, and baking powder and gently fold into above mixture. Stir melted butter into egg/flour mixture gently. Do not deflate the batter by overmixing.

Bake in a 10-inch springform pan for 30 minutes. Watch cake carefully, for it will sink in the center if it overbakes. It is done when it springs back if lightly touched in the center. Immediately remove from the oven and cool upside down on a cake rack. It is easiest to work with when completely cooled and/or refrigerated.

HAZELNUT LIQUEUR MIXTURE

1 cup confectioners' sugar
¹/₃ cup hazelnut liqueur
1 tablespoon vanilla
³/₄ cup hot water

Mix ingredients thoroughly and pour into a bottle with spray nozzle.

HAZELNUT FILLING

¹/₂ cup butter, softened
¹/₂ cup cream cheese, softened
1 cup confectioners' sugar
Vanilla flavoring

¹/₄ cup cornstarch
¹/₂ cup sugar
2 cups milk
1 egg yolk
1 teaspoon vanilla

2 ounces semi-sweet chocolate, melted
1 cup toasted, ground hazelnuts
1 cup whipped cream

Cream butter and cream cheese together. Gradually add confectioners' sugar, and beat until light and fluffy. Add vanilla to taste. Set aside.

Mix cornstarch, sugar, and milk in a medium saucepan. Whisk thoroughly to remove lumps. Cook over high heat until mixture thickens. Remove from heat and beat thoroughly with a wire whisk. Whisk in egg yolk and vanilla. Return to heat until mixture is quite thick.

Remove from heat and combine with butter/cream cheese mixture. Cool quickly in refrigerator.

When custard mixture is cool, mix together with melted chocolate and hazelnuts. Fold in whipped cream.

TO ASSEMBLE TORTE

Divide the sponge into three to four layers. Beginning with the base layer, spray it liberally with Hazelnut Liqueur Mixture, then spread on a coat of Hazelnut Filling. Spray the second layer with Liqueur Mixture spread a coat of plain sweetened whipped cream on it. Using a sheet of plastic wrap to help you, carefully place second layer on top of base, with whipped cream side DOWN. Repeat this process with each additional layer. Cover top and sides of torte with Hazelnut Filling. Pour a layer of melted chocolate over top and sides. Refrigerate for several hours or overnight before serving.

Garnish with sweetened whipped cream.

TORTE A LA KNUTZEN

This elegant custard torte topped with fresh sweet cherries comes from my Aunt Marcia Knutzen. The torte and the custard may be made a day ahead of time and stored separately, then put together with whipped cream and cherries just before serving.

TORTE

3 egg whites
1 cup sugar
1 teaspoon vinegar

Line a 9-inch round or square pan with waxed paper.

Beat egg whites until stiff. Add sugar slowly, then add vinegar. Pour mixture into prepared pan. Place in a cold oven, and turn oven on to 325 degrees. Bake for about 1 hour. Remove torte from pan immediately.

CUSTARD

3 egg yolks
1/2 cup sugar
2 tablespoons flour
Pinch salt
1 tablespoon milk
2 cups milk
1 tablespoon butter
1 teaspoon vanilla
2 bananas

In a small bowl, mix egg yolks, sugar, flour, salt, and about 1 table-spoon of milk for a thickening.

In top of double boiler, scald 2 cups milk. Add egg mixture and stir with a wooden spoon over medium-low heat until mixture thickly coats back of spoon. Do not allow to boil. Remove from heat and add butter and vanilla. Set aside to cool. Slice bananas into the custard when cooled and spread on torte.

TOPPING

1 pint sweetened whipped cream
Fresh sweet cherries

Top torte with whipped cream and fresh sweet cherries.

Scrumptious
SWEETS

APPLE IMPROMPTU

A tasty and versatile dessert from "The Dairy Family of the Year, 1985."
Erin Moe advises that this recipe adapts beautifully to other fruits and
berries, especially rhubarb. If there's any left over, it's wonderful cold for
a slightly sinful breakfast.

> *4 cups sliced apples*
> *1/4 cup sugar*
> *1/4 teaspoon cinnamon*
>
> *3/4 cup sugar*
> *3/4 cup butter*
> *1 large egg*
> *1 1/2 teaspoons vanilla*
> *3/4 cup flour*
> *3/4 teaspoon baking powder*
>
> *Garnish: whipped cream*

Preheat oven to 400 degrees.

Arrange apple slices in a 9-inch greased pan or pie plate. Sprinkle
with 1/4 cup sugar and 1/4 teaspoon of cinnamon. Cover with foil and
bake for 20 minutes.

While apples are baking, cream together 3/4 cup sugar and butter.
Add egg and vanilla and beat well. Stir in flour and baking powder.
When apples have baked for 20 minutes, remove from oven and spread
topping mixture over all. Return to oven and bake for 20-25 more minutes, until golden brown. Let cool for 5-10 minutes before serving. Garnish with whipped cream.

4-6 portions

BLUEBERRY BUCKLE

Another prizewinner from the Samish Island Road Run Potluck.

3/4 cup sugar
1/4 cup butter, softened
1 egg, beaten
1/2 cup milk
2 cups flour
2 teaspoons baking powder
1/2 teaspoon salt
1/2 teaspoon cinnamon
1 cup blueberries

TOPPING

1/2 cup sugar
1/3 cup flour
1/4 teaspoon nutmeg
1/4 cup butter

Preheat oven to 375 degrees. Grease and flour a 9-inch square pan.

In a large mixing bowl, cream butter and sugar. Add egg and milk and blend well. Sift together flour, baking powder, salt, and cinnamon. Gradually add to creamed mixture, mixing well. Fold in berries. Pour into prepared pan.

Combine topping ingredients in a small bowl. Sprinkle over batter. Bake for 45 to 50 minutes.

LEMON SAUCE

1/2 cup butter
1 cup sugar
1 1/4 cups water
1 egg, beaten
3 tablespoons lemon juice
1 tablespoon lemon peel, grated

Preheat broiler.

Melt butter in a medium saucepan. Add sugar, water, and beaten egg. Bring to a boil, remove from heat, and stir in lemon juice and lemon peel. Pierce cake with toothpick in a few places and pour a portion of the sauce over cake. Broil briefly until bubbly and golden. Serve warm or cold with remaining sauce.

KRISTINA KRINGLE

Once a Christmas gift from Gretchen, this almond pastry flaking with flavor is well worth making all year round.

1 cup flour
1/2 cup butter
2 tablespoons water

1 cup water
1/2 cup butter
1 cup flour
3 eggs
1/2 teaspoon salt
1/2 teaspoon almond extract

Preheat oven to 375 degrees.

Cut together 1 cup of flour and 1/2 cup of butter until mixture resembles fine meal. Add water and blend well. Form dough into a ball and divide in half. Using the heel of your hand, press dough into two 3-inch wide strips down the length of a cookie sheet.

In a saucepan, bring 1 cup of water and 1/2 cup of butter to a boil. Remove from heat. Add flour, and stir until smooth. Add eggs one at a time, blending well after each addition. Add salt and extract. Spread on top of dough strips.

Bake for 45 minutes. Cool and frost with Almond Icing.

ALMOND ICING

1/4 cup butter, softened
1 cup confectioners' sugar
1 tablespoon milk
1/2 teaspoon almond extract

Combine the butter, sugar, milk, and extract. Blend until smooth and spread over pastry.

OLEBOLLEN

These deep fried balls of sweet dough are an old Dutch recipe from "Wooden Shoes."

3 ¹/₄ cups all-purpose flour
2 packages active dry yeast
1 cup milk
¹/₃ cup sugar
¹/₄ cup butter
1 teaspoon salt
1 teaspoon vanilla
2 eggs
3 egg yolks
¹/₂ cup raisins
¹/₂ cup apples, chopped fine

Oil

¹/₂ cup sugar
1 teaspoon ground cinnamon

In a large bowl, combine 2 cups of flour and yeast. Set aside.

In a saucepan, heat milk, ¹/₃ cup sugar, butter, and salt just until warm, stirring constantly. Stir in vanilla. Add to flour mixture. Add eggs and egg yolks. Beat at low speed on an electric mixer for ¹/₂ minute, scraping bowl. Beat on high speed for 3 minutes.

Stir in rest of flour, raisins, and apples. Cover and let rise until double, about 30 minutes.

Heat oil in a deep fat fryer to 375 degrees. Carefully drop batter by tablespoons into hot oil and fry for about 3 minutes, turning to brown on all sides. Drain well on paper towels. While still warm, dust with a mixture of ¹/₂ cup sugar and cinnamon.

36 balls

Olebollen

BAY VIEW APPLE BLOSSOMS

In the late 1800's, the growing community of Bay View boasted a school, a Methodist church, a post office, a store, and two mills. All was flourishing until New Year's Day, 1910, when a fire destroyed most of the buildings. Today Bay View is known for its waterfront park, the Breazeale-Padilla Bay Interpretive Center and wildlife sanctuary, Rozema's Boatworks, and Merritt's Apple Orchards. The Merritts farm some 25 acres of Washington apples, with the old-fashioned green Gravenstein as their mainstay. They wash, sort, pack, and sell directly from their orchard. Enjoy a Saturday drive and come home with a crisp bite of the valley.

1 cup finely ground tart apples, preferably Gravensteins
2 cups granulated sugar
2 envelopes unflavored gelatin
1 tablespoon water
1/2 cup finely ground nuts
Confectioners' sugar

Grind peeled apples in a food grinder. Combine apples and sugar in a saucepan and bring to a boil over low heat. Stir to prevent sticking and boil for 1 minute; reduce to a simmer for 15-20 minutes, until quite thick and clear.

Meanwhile, soak gelatin in 1 tablespoon of water, stirring to dissolve. Add gelatin to hot apple mixture and mix until granules are completely dissolved. Add nuts.

Pour into a small greased pan. Score the apple mixture into small squares while still pliable. Let stand for 8-12 hours. Cut and remove from pan and roll in confectioners' sugar. Lay sugared squares on waxed paper to dry further. Store in a metal container in a cool, dry place.

Bay View — 1910.

MELON ICE

A pretty pastel fruit ice from the Rhododendron Cafe.

1 cantalope
1 honeydew melon
1/4 watermelon
2 cups Gewurtztraminer
2 1/4 cups sugar
1 tablespoon lemon juice

Puree meat from cantalope, honeydew, and watermelon in blender or food processor. Strain through a wire strainer, reserving juice. Measure out 7 cups juice.

Blend Gewurtztraminer, sugar, and lemon juice with melon juice. Freeze in an ice cream freezer according to instructions or place in ice cube trays overnight and puree in food processor or blender and refreeze after pureed smooth. Spoon into individual sherbet glasses to serve.

BLUEBERRY ICE

A simple dessert or sorbet.

4 cups blueberries
1 1/4 cups sugar
1 1/4 cups water
3 tablespoons fresh lemon juice
Dash of salt
Dash of cinnamon
3 egg whites, at room temperature

Garnish: Fresh mint sprigs

Puree blueberries. In a saucepan, combine sugar and water and bring to a boil. Set aside to cool. Add berry puree, lemon juice, salt, and cinnamon. Blend well. Pour into an ungreased 9-inch square pan.

Freeze uncovered until solid (2-3 hours). Remove from freezer. In a small bowl, beat egg whites until stiff. Then beat blueberry mixture until smooth and light in color. Beat in one-fourth of the egg whites, and then fold in the remaining.

Cover and return to freezer. To serve, scoop into small dishes and garnish with fresh mint.

BERRY KREM

This can be made from any berry—blackberry, huckleberry, blueberry, or grape. "Krem" in Swedish likely comes from the French "creme," a dessert made by thickening and sweetening liquids.

To 4 parts of berries add 1 part water and bring to a boil. Simmer for 20 to 25 minutes. Strain juice through a wire strainer or food mill, but do not force pulp through. To every 2 cups of juice, add ½ cup of sugar and thicken with 1 level tablespoon of corn starch dissolved in ¼ cup water. Sweetening and thickening may be adjusted to your taste. Serve hot or cold with a bit of whipped cream.

ZABAGLIONE

A refreshing way to dress up fresh berries of all sorts. Compliments of The Oyster Bar.

1 quart fresh blackberries, raspberries, strawberries or blueberries

1 teaspoon unflavored gelatin
1 cup sweet Marsala
7 egg yolks
³/₄ cup sugar
Zest from ¹/₂ lemon
¹/₃ teaspoon cinnamon
¹/₂ teaspoon vanilla
1 cup whipping cream

Dissolve gelatin in ½ cup of the Marsala and melt over a double boiler. Set aside.

Combine yolks, sugar, and remaining ½ cup of Marsala in a mixing bowl. Place over hot water and beat hard until it is hot. Do not overcook. Transfer to an electric mixer and beat until cool and thick. Add lemon zest, cinnamon, gelatin mixture, and vanilla. Transfer to a large bowl.

Whip cream until stiff, then fold into egg mixture. Pour over fresh fruit and chill.

2 cups

KAN IKKE LA VAERE

This Scandinavian dessert is a Christmas Eve tradition in our family. Its name means "cannot leave it alone," and it is well-deserved.

1 tablespoon plain gelatin
1/2 cup cold water
5 eggs, separated
3/4 cup sugar
Juice and grated rind of 1 medium lemon

Garnish:
Sweetened whipped cream
Maraschino cherries

Soak gelatin in cold water for 5 minutes, then place in a double boiler over boiling water. Stir until completely dissolved. Remove from heat and cool to lukewarm.

Beat egg whites stiff, and set aside. Beat egg yolks, and gradually add sugar. Beat until they are smooth and form a ribbon. Add lemon juice and grated rind. Add cooled gelatin. Fold in egg whites. Chill until set. Serve in sherbet glasses garnished with whipped cream and a maraschino cherry.

8 portions

SWEDISH CREAM

The Skagit Valley is one of the largest dairy farming areas in Washington. Phyllis Moe combines several of our local dairy products in this splendid dessert.

> 2 cups whipping cream
> 1 cup milk
> 1/2 cup sugar
> 1/4 teaspoon salt
> 2 envelopes Knox gelatin
> 1/4 cup cold water
> 1 teaspoon vanilla
> 2 cups sour cream

Heat cream, milk, sugar, and salt in a large saucepan until lukewarm. Stir until sugar dissolves.

Dissolve gelatin in cold water and set over hot water until clear. Add to cream mixture. When the mixture has cooled and is beginning to congeal, add vanilla and fold in sour cream. Pour into a mold or 9-inch pan. Continue to cool and serve with Raspberry Sauce.

RASPBERRY SAUCE

> 1 pint frozen sweetened raspberries, or 1 1/2 pints fresh
> 2 tablespoons cornstarch

If using frozen berries, thaw completely and drain off syrup into a measuring cup. Add enough water to make 2 cups of liquid. If using fresh berries, puree about 1 cup of berries in blender. Add 3-4 tablespoons of sugar to taste and enough water to make 2 cups.

Combine berry liquid with cornstarch and cook for about 2 minutes over medium heat, until thickened. Remove from heat and add whole berries.

milk wagon
Mount Vernon 1910.

ENGLISH PUDDING

This classic pudding with its own rich sauce is an old recipe from my Grandma Betty Houser, Sr. It will warm your heart when served on cold winter nights.

1 tablespoon butter
1/2 cup white sugar
1/2 cup milk
1 cup flour
1 teaspoon baking soda
1/8 teaspoon salt
1/2 cup dates, coarsely chopped
1/2 cup walnuts, coarsely chopped

1 cup brown sugar
2 cups water
2 tablespoons butter

Garnish: sweetened whipped cream

Preheat oven to 350 degrees. Lightly oil a 10 X 9-inch oblong pan.

In a bowl, blend butter and sugar. Stir in milk. Add flour, soda, and salt, then dates and nuts. Pour into prepared pan and set aside.

In a medium saucepan, combine brown sugar, water, and butter. Bring to a boil while stirring constantly. Pour hot over batter in pan. Bake for 30 minutes.

Let cool slightly before cutting into squares. Invert onto dessert plates, and spoon sauce over the top. Serve warm with sweetened whipped cream.

DATE NUT PUDDING

I first tasted this warm and wonderful dessert while visiting my Grandma Ellen in the city on a chilly December day. The recipe is from my great-grandmother, Laura Wilkinson. Be sure to buy fresh dates from the produce market; boxed dates will not give the desired results.

2 eggs
1 cup sugar
1 pinch of salt
2 tablespoons flour
2 teaspoons baking powder
1 1/2 pound dates, chopped
1 pound walnuts, chopped

Garnish: whipped cream

Preheat oven to 325 degrees.

Beat eggs. Add sugar, salt, flour, baking powder, and blend well. Add dates and nuts. Spread about 1/2" thick in 11 X 7-inch pan. Bake for 30 minutes.

Cut into squares and serve warm with whipped cream. These should be served toasty warm – they may be reheated if necessary.

RIZOGALO

A Greek rice pudding with a zest of lemon.

1 quart milk
1/3 cup rice
1/3 cup sugar
1/2 teaspoon salt
1 teaspoon vanilla
1/2 cup cream
1/2 cup raisins

Garnish: freshly grated lemon rind

In a heavy medium saucepan, slowly heat milk over low heat. Add rice, sugar, and salt, and cook for 45 minutes, stirring occasionally. Add vanilla and cream and raisins. Cool. Spoon into individual serving dishes and garnish with fresh lemon peel.

RICE IMPERATRICE WITH CHERRY SAUCE

This elegant mold is especially colorful at Christmas.

1/2 cup uncooked rice
2 cups water
2 1/2 cups milk
1 envelope unflavored gelatin
1/4 cup cold water
2 eggs
1/2 cup sugar
1 teaspoon vanilla
1 cup cream, whipped

Cook rice in 2 cups of water for 30 minutes or until all the water is absorbed. Add 1 1/4 cups milk; simmer 30 minutes or until milk is absorbed. Set aside to cool.

Soften gelatin in cold water.

Beat eggs lightly in top of double boiler; add sugar and remaining 1 1/4 cups milk. Cook over simmering water, stirring constantly, until mixture coats spoon. Add vanilla and gelatin; stir until gelatin is dissolved. Turn into a large bowl and stir in the rice.

Chill custard mixture, stirring often, until it starts to thicken. Fold in whipped cream. Turn into 6 or 8-cup mold. Refrigerate 3 hours and unmold onto serving platter. Top with Cherry Sauce.

CHERRY SAUCE

1 pint jar of homemade cherry preserves, or cherry pie filling
2 tablespoons brandy (optional)

Reserve a few cherries for garnish. Whirl remainder in blender until smooth. If desired, stir in brandy and a few drops of red food coloring. Chill well before serving.

10 portions

CARAMEL FLAN

A delicate custard.

³/4 cup sugar

2 cups milk
2 cups light cream
6 eggs
¹/2 cup sugar
¹/2 teaspoon salt
2 teaspoons vanilla extract

Heat a 8-inch round, shallow baking dish in oven.

Place ³/4 cup sugar in a skillet and cook over medium heat until sugar melts and forms a light brown syrup. Stir to blend. Pour syrup into heated baking dish. Holding dish with pot holders, quickly rotate to cover bottom and sides. Set dish aside.

Preheat oven to 325 degrees.

In a medium saucepan, heat milk and cream until bubbles form around the edge of pan. Set aside.

In a large bowl, beat eggs slightly with rotary beater. Add sugar, salt, and vanilla. Gradually stir in hot milk mixture. Pour into prepared dish on top of caramelized sugar.

Set dish in a shallow pan and pour boiling water to ¹/2-inch level around dish. Bake for 35-40 minutes, until knife inserted in center comes out clean. Let custard cool, then refrigerate 4 hours or overnight.

To serve, run a small spatula around edge of dish to loosen. Invert on serving dish and shake gently to release. The caramel acts as a sauce.

CAPIROTADA

This Mexican bread pudding is traditionally served during Lent. Anita Guillen gave me the recipe along with these memories: "To this day the flavor of this dish reminds me of my Grandmother's kitchen. I clearly recall watching with delight as she assembled the ingredients into the dish. I saw her hands move with flawless grace following the recipe she had kept in her head, a simple but richly satisfying pudding of stale bread, raisins, and cheese. Time has not taken away these memories."

> 3 1/2 cups water
> 4 cinnamon sticks
> 10 1/2-inch slices French bread or any stale white bread
> 1 cup brown sugar
> 2 cups grated cheese
> 1 cup raisins
>
> Garnish: whipped cream flavored with rum

Boil cinnamon sticks in water over high heat for ten minutes. Keep warm. In a 2 1/2-quart baking dish, layer five slices of bread. Cut the slices if necessary to fill spaces evenly. Sprinkle with 1/2 cup of brown sugar, one cup of the grated cheese, and 1/2 cup of the raisins. Cover the mixture with the remaining bread and sprinkle the remaining raisins over the top. Discard cinnamon sticks and pour 1 cup of the hot liquid over bread mixture. Add the rest of the cheese and top with remaining 1/2 cup of sugar.

Cover and let stand until liquid is absorbed (about 15 minutes). Run a spoon or a knife along the side of the dish. If the bread looks dry, pour in the rest of the cinnamon liquid.

Preheat oven to 350 degrees.

Bake, covered, for 30 minutes. Serve at once with rum-flavored whipped cream.

cinnamon.

FRANGOS

Decadent chocolate creams.

1 cup butter, softened
2 cups confectioners' sugar
16 ounces semi-sweet chocolate, melted
4 eggs
1 teaspoon peppermint flavoring
2 teaspoons vanilla
2 cups Graham cracker crumbs or vanilla wafer crumbs

Garnish: maraschino cherries

Cream butter and sugar. Add melted chocolate. Beat until mixed well. Beat in eggs. Add peppermint and vanilla flavorings and blend well.

Line muffin tins with paper liners. Sprinkle bottom of each cup liner with crumbs. Spoon in chocolate mixture or pipe mixture into cup using frosting bag and tip. Sprinkle additional crumbs on top. Place in freezer until firm. Garnish with a maraschino cherry on each frango.

COOKIE
Classics

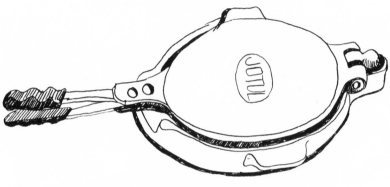

Krumkager iron

KRUMKAGER

A light, crisp Scandinavian cookie baked in a pretty cone shape. We always serve these at Christmas and at weddings.

> 1 cup butter, melted
> 2 cups sugar
> 4 eggs and 2 egg yolks, beaten
> 1 cup cream
> 1 teaspoon cardamom
> 4 cups unbleached all-purpose flour

Cream butter and sugar. Add beaten eggs. Add cream, then gradually add flour sifted with cardamom. Drop by teaspoons onto a hot krumkager iron and bake until lightly browned on both sides. Remove from iron and immediately roll into a cone or cylinder.

PFEFFERNUSSE

When your neighbors drop by, enjoy these peppernuts with a cup of fresh coffee.

>2 cups brown sugar
>1 cup white sugar
>3 eggs
>1 1/4 teaspoons soda
>1 1/2 tablespoons hot water
>3 teaspoons cinnamon
>1 1/2 teaspoons cardamom
>1/2 teaspoon fresh fine ground black pepper
>2 cups ground nuts
>4 1/2 cups sifted unbleached all-purpose flour

Preheat oven to 350 degrees.

In a large bowl, combine sugars and eggs. In a small bowl, dissolve soda in hot water and add to sugar/egg mixture. Stir in cinnamon, cardamom, and pepper. Fold in nuts, then add flour gradually. The dough will be very stiff. Carefully roll out dough and cut with a circular cookie cutter.

Bake for 12 to 15 minutes. Transfer to cookie racks and dust with confectioners' sugar. Cool and store in airtight containers.

AYERSHIRE SHORTBREAD

A Scottish tradition, these are a crisp and flaky treat.

>1 cup sugar
>1/2 cup brown or white rice flour
>4 1/2 cups unbleached all-purpose flour
>1 pound butter, softened

Preheat oven to 300 degrees.

Mix together sugar, rice flour, and unbleached flour until combined well. Add dry ingredients gradually to softened butter, working with a spoon. When the mixture becomes too stiff, knead in the remainder of the dry ingredients by hand until you have a soft, well-mixed dough.

With your hands, pat the dough out until it is about 1/2 inch thick on a cookie sheet. Prick with a fork and bake for 45 minutes to 1 hour.

MONKEY BARS

A luscious lemon treat from the Monkey Business.

>1 cup unbleached flour
>1/4 cup confectioners' sugar
>1/2 cup butter
>
>2 eggs
>1 cup sugar
>2 tablespoons flour
>1 tablespoon grated lemon rind
>1/2 teaspoon baking powder
>2 tablespoons lemon juice

Preheat oven to 350 degrees.

Combine 1 cup of flour and confectioners' sugar in a mixing bowl. Cut in butter until the mixture is crumbly. Press flour mixture into an 8 or 9-inch square pan. Bake for 15-18 minutes.

In a small bowl, beat eggs and sugar until light in color; stir in 2 tablespoons of flour, lemon rind, baking powder, and lemon juice. Pour over baked crust and return to oven for 18-20 minutes, until light golden brown. Cool completely. If desired, sprinkle with confectioners' sugar. Cut into bars.

18-24 bars

SHORTBREAD CUTOUTS

Cutouts say a thousand words in a cookie. Heart shapes for someone special, shell shapes for the beach party, dog and cat shapes for rainy days. They will all melt in your mouth.

>1 cup butter
>1/2 cup confectioners' sugar
>2 cups sifted unbleached all-purpose flour

Preheat oven to 350 degrees.

Cream butter thoroughly. Blend in sugar and mix thoroughly. Add flour gradually, then knead to blend well. Roll out to 1/4-inch thickness on a lightly floured board. Cut into shapes with cookie cutters or into 2-inch squares.

Bake on an ungreased baking sheet for 8-10 minutes, until cookies are a delicate golden color. Cool on cake racks.

3 dozen cookies

VALENTINE HEARTS

My Grandma Knutzen stole my heart with these cookies.

> *2/3 cup butter*
> *1 1/2 cups sugar*
> *2 eggs, slightly beaten*
> *3 cups flour, sifted*
> *1 teaspoon salt*
> *2 teaspoons baking powder*
> *Juice and grated rind of 1 orange*

Preheat oven to 350 degrees.

Cream butter and sugar. Add eggs and beat well. Gradually add flour, salt, and baking powder. Add orange juice and rind. Cover dough and chill.

Roll dough out on lightly floured board and cut out heart shapes. Place on baking sheet and bake for 5-8 minutes, until light brown. Cool on wire racks, then give your hearts away.

SMOR BULLAR

These "butter balls" are the Scandinavian version of Mexican wedding cakes and Russian teacakes.

> *1 cup butter*
> *1/2 cup confectioners' sugar*
> *2 1/4 cups sifted cake flour*
> *1/4 teaspoon salt*
> *1 teaspoon vanilla*
> *3/4 cups pecans, chopped fine*

Preheat oven to 400 degrees.

Cream butter and sugar thoroughly. Add flour, salt, vanilla, and pecans and mix well. Cover dough and chill.

Roll dough into small balls, and place 2 inches apart on an ungreased baking sheet. Bake until set, but do not brown. Roll in confectioners' sugar while warm. When cool, roll again in confectioners' sugar.

ANN'S ALMOND BARS

A Dutch delight from Ann Voorde Poorte.

> 2 cups oatmeal
> 1 cup brown sugar
> 1 cup butter
> 2 cups unbleached all-purpose flour
> 1/2 teaspoon salt
> 1/2 teaspoon baking soda

> FILLING

> 2 cups sugar
> 4 egg yolks
> 3/4 cup flour
> 1/2 cup milk
> 6 teaspoons almond flavoring

Preheat oven to 350 degrees.

Combine oatmeal, brown sugar, butter, flour, salt, and soda in a large mixing bowl and work together until the mixture reaches a crumbly texture. Put half of this mixture in 9 X 13-inch baking dish. Mix filling and spread over mixture. Top with remaining crumb mix.

Bake for 30 minutes. Cool and cut into bars.

FATTIGMAND

These are traditional Scandinavian cookies; their name means "poor man". Families who had little else still had a cow to give cream and chickens who laid eggs.

> 6 egg yolks
> 6 tablespoons sugar
> 6 tablespoons sweet cream
> 1 tablespoon melted butter
> 3 cups unbleached all-purpose flour
> 1/8 teaspoon cardamom
> 1/8 teaspoon salt

Beat eggs well, then add sugar and beat until thick and yellow. Mix in cream and butter. Add flour mixed with cardamom and salt and combine thoroughly. Roll out thin and cut into diamond shapes.

Fry in deep fat at 370 degrees for 2-3 minutes, until golden brown. Dust with confectioners' sugar.

BUTTER KUCHEN

Delightful almond tarts.

> *1 cup butter*
> *2 cups unbleached all-purpose flour*
> *1 egg*
> *2 tablespoons cold water*

FILLING

> *8 ounces almond paste*
> *1³/₄ cups confectioners' sugar*
> *1 egg white*
> *2 tablespoons water*

Preheat oven to 425 degrees.

Cut butter into flour with a pastry blender until the mixture is the size of small peas. Beat the egg and water together and blend into the flour/butter mixture. Knead dough lightly. On a lightly floured board, roll the dough into a 12 X 15-inch rectangle and fold dough into thirds. Roll out again. Repeat this folding and rolling operation two more times. Roll dough the final time to a ¹/₄-inch thickness. Cut into 2¹/₂-inch rounds. Place pastry rounds in a 2-inch muffin pan.

Combine almond paste and sugar until the mixture resembles the texture of cornmeal. Beat the egg white until it is foamy. Add the water to the eggwhite and continue beating until soft peaks form. Fold the egg white in with the almond paste and sugar.

Fill each pastry round with one teaspoon of almond filling. Bake for 5 minutes at 425 degrees. Lower oven temperature to 350 degrees, and continue baking for another 9-12 minutes.

3-4 dozen cookies

TOAST
Masters

GREEK COFFEE

A very fine ground dark roasted coffee that is traditionally brewed in a "briki," a small brass coffee pot. This coffee may also be brewed in a very small, deep saucepan. Greek coffee may be purchased at Greek specialty shops. I use a brand called Venizelos.

Measure one demitasse cup of cold water for each cup desired and pour into "briki." Bring water to a simmer. Add one heaping teaspoon each of coffee and sugar for each cup. Stir. The amount of sugar may be varied. Bring liquid to a boil over a low flame, until a creamy foam is formed. Remove from heat. Divide amount of foam into each cup, and fill cups with remaining coffee. Do not stir coffee in cups as the rather muddy grounds settle and are not for drinking.

MAY WINE

A celebration of spring. The sweet woodruff grows just outside Lavonne's kitchen step. This wine is extra special when the white flowers are blossoming. Plant some sweet woodruff and start your own springtime tradition.

> *3 liters of Rhine wine*
> *¹/2 cup sweet woodruff, new growth*
> *1 orange, sliced*
> *1 lemon, sliced*
> *1 cup strawberries, sliced*

Combine the wine, sweet woodruff, and sliced fruit. Serve in a big punch bowl in the backyard while your guests enjoy the new spring air.

STRAWBERRY BAY FIZZ

A strawberry refresher. When the sun is hot and high in the sky, sit in your lawn chair and enjoy the essence of summer.

> *6 ounces frozen limeade concentrate*
> *4 shots (1¹/2 ounces each) rum or Tequila (6 ounces total)*
> *1 tablespoon Rose's lime juice*
> *2 cups fresh or frozen strawberries*
> *2-3 cups (about 14) ice cubes*
>
> *Garnish: fresh lime slices*

In blender, combine above ingredients in order written. Process until smooth. Serve in chilled glasses garnished with lime slices.

4 portions

RASPBERRY SEASON DAIQUIRI

> *4 cups fresh or frozen raspberries*
> *¹/3 to ¹/2 cup sugar*
> *6-ounce can frozen lemonade concentrate*
> *4 cups crushed ice*
> *1 cup light rum*

Combine raspberries with sugar, lemonade, ice, and rum in blender. Whirl until smooth. Spoon into large glasses and serve immediately.

4-6 portions

SANGRIA

¹/₂ gallon Spanish red wine
¹/₃ cup sugar
¹/₃ cup brandy
3 large oranges
2 large lemons
¹/₄ cup Triple Sec
1 cup club soda

Pour wine into punch bowl. Add sugar and brandy. Squeeze juice from 2 oranges and 1 lemon into bowl. Add fruit. Chill about 1 hour. Remove fruit and slice remaining orange and lemon thinly and add to punch. Stir in Triple Sec and club soda and serve.

RASPBERRY CORDIAL

Cordially yours from Darlene Hamburg, who farms raspberries on Riverbend Road. This ruby drink will save the essence of fresh raspberries to taste in cold December.

1 quart raspberries
1 quart vodka
1 pound sugar

Combine raspberries, vodka, and sugar and stir well. Store in a dark, cool place for about 6 weeks. Turn or rotate daily. Filter and bottle. Store in a dark, cool place.

BACKYARD BLACKBERRY BRANDY

Begin with the prolific Northwest roadside blackberries. If they're not in your backyard, take a Sunday drive and a pail.

2 cups sugar cubes
2 cups blackberries
Vodka

Fill a quart jar with blackberries and sugar cubes. Pour vodka in until jar is ³/₄ full. Seal tightly. Invert jar daily for 6 weeks. Strain mixture through cheesecloth into a sterile bottle and store another six weeks before drinking.

HOT APPLE PIE

This drink is full of warm spicy aroma and taste; it brings back memories of pressing cider in the fall.

> *1 quart apple cider*
> *4 cloves, whole*
> *4 ounces Tuaca*
>
> *Garnish: whipped cream*
> *4 cinnamon sticks*

Bring apple cider and cloves to a boil. Pour 1¼ ounces of Tuaca into stemmed 8-ounce glasses. Strain cider into glasses within ½ inch of rim. Top with whipped cream and garnish with cinnamon sticks.

4 portions

KAHLUA

> *5 cups strong coffee*
> *1½ cups brown sugar*
> *1½ cups white sugar*
> *One fifth of 100 proof vodka*
> *2 vanilla beans*

Brew five cups of very strong coffee, preferably with fresh ground beans. Combine coffee and sugars. Simmer for about 1 hour until syrupy. It should coat a spoon. Let cool. Add vodka and vanilla beans. Store in a capped bottle for 30 days. Rotate bottle daily to avoid settling.

HOT BUTTERED RUM

To warm a rainy Northwest evening.

> *2 pounds brown sugar*
> *2 pounds butter*
> *½ gallon vanilla ice cream*
> *Rum*
> *Nutmeg*

Cream butter and sugar together. Blend in ice cream and store in freezer until ready to use.

To serve, put 2 heaping teaspoons of batter into a mug. Add a shot of rum. Fill cup with hot water and sprinkle with freshly grated nutmeg.

PANTRY
Pleasures

ANCHOVY BUTTER

¹/₂ cup unsalted butter, at room temperature
4 anchovy fillets, drained and chopped
1 tablespoon fresh lemon juice
Dash hot pepper sauce

Combine all ingredients in small bowl and mix well.

1 ¹/₂ cups

BASIL BUTTER

A perfect dressing for homemade pasta, especially when your fresh basil is flourishing.

¹/₂ cup unsalted butter, room temperature
2 tablespoons fresh basil
1 teaspoon tomato paste
1 clove garlic, pressed
Freshly ground pepper

Combine all ingredients in a small bowl and mix well.

1 ¹/₂ cups

HORSERADISH BUTTER

We keep a patch of horseradish in our Alice Bay garden. It's easy to grow and use. It makes a lusty companion to a grilled T-bone steak, swathed over tender carrots, or spread on a rich, crusty bread.

¹/₂ cup butter, at room temperature
2 tablespoons grated horseradish
1 teaspoon lemon juice

Combine all ingredients and blend well.

¹/₂ cup

CREME FRAICHE

Here are two versions of a kitchen staple. See which one you like best, then keep some on hand for soups, sauces, and fruit.

The first is a tart, tangy mixture, good for soups and sauces.

> *1 cup heavy cream*
> *1 cup buttermilk*

Combine cream and buttermilk in a jar. Shake mixture vigorously for 1 minute. Let stand at room temperature at least 8 hours, until thick. Store in refrigerator. Will keep for 4 weeks.

This second version has a richer taste. I use it over fresh fruits and berries and over steamed vegetables.

> *1 cup heavy cream*
> *1 cup sour cream*

Whisk cream and sour cream together. Cover loosely and let stand in a warm spot in the kitchen overnight or until thickened. Cover and store in the refrigerator for up to two weeks. As this heavy cream sits it develops a delicate sour taste.

BLUEBERRY CONSERVE

> *2 cups water*
> *4 cups sugar*
> *1/2 lemon, thinly sliced*
> *1/2 orange, thinly sliced*
> *1/2 cup seedless raisins*
> *1 quart stemmed blueberries*

Bring water and sugar to a boil. Add lemon, orange, and raisins. Simmer for 5 minutes. Add blueberries and cook rapidly until thick, about 30 minutes. As mixture thickens, stir frequently to prevent sticking. Pour boiling hot mixture into sterilized jars. Adjust caps.

2 pints

APPLE CHUTNEY

A complement to pork and poultry; also a welcome gift.

> 8 cups tart apples, peeled and chopped
> 4¹/₂ cups sugar
> 2 cups seedless golden raisins
> 1 cup coarsely chopped toasted pecans or walnuts
> ¹/₂ cup vinegar
> Peel of 2 oranges, coarsely grated
> ¹/₃ teaspoon cloves

Combine all ingredients in large heavy kettle. Place over high heat and bring to a rolling boil, stirring constantly. Reduce heat to a simmer and cook slowly until apples are tender and syrup is very thick and almost caramelized. Ladle into hot steriliized jars, seal, and store in a cool, dark, dry place.

Keep refrigerated after opening.

3¹/₂ pints

SPICED APPLE MARMALADE

> 12 inches of cinnamon sticks
> ¹/₂ teaspoon whole cloves
> 6 cardamom pods, cracked
> 1 fresh lemon, unpeeled, quartered, seeds removed, thinly sliced
> 6 medium apples (6 cups), peeled, cored, finely chopped
> 2 cups water
> ¹/₄ cup orange juice
> 5 cups sugar

Combine the spices in a cheesecloth bag.

In a large, 8-10 quart kettle, combine spices, lemon slices, apples, water, and orange juice. Bring to a boil. Reduce heat and simmer until apples are tender, about 10 minutes. Remove spice bag. Add sugar. Bring mixture to a full rolling boil, stirring constantly. Boil for 15 minutes, until the mixture is thick and clear, or until it sheets when poured from a metal spoon. Remove from heat and skim off foam. Pour at once into hot, sterile jars. Wipe jar rims clean and seal.

3 pints

RASPBERRY RELISH

2 cups raspberries
1 cup cranberries
1¹/₂ cups sugar

Bring cranberries to a boil. Add sugar and stir until completely dissolved. Add raspberries and simmer for 3 minutes.

Serve with pork, poultry, or fish.

RASPBERRY SAUCE

A lovely finishing touch for poultry or pork.

10 ounces fresh or frozen raspberries
2 tablespoons dry white wine
1 tablespoon orange liqueur
2 teaspoons cornstarch
1 tablespoon butter

Place fresh or thawed raspberries in blender container and blend until smooth. In a medium saucepan, combine wine, orange liquer, and cornstarch. Stir in raspberries and butter. Cook, stirring constantly, until mixture is thickened and bubbly. Cook and stir for 2 minutes more. Strain through a sieve and serve warm.

BLUEBERRY SYRUP

What a treat for pancakes and aebelskiver.

2 quarts ripe blueberries
3¹/₂ cups water
4¹/₂ cups sugar

Crush berries and combine with water in a heavy kettle. Bring to a boil and boil rapidly for 10 minutes. Lower heat and simmer for 5 more minutes. Strain juice through jelly bag and measure. You should have about 5 cups of juice.

Add sugar to juice and boil rapidly for 12 minutes until syrup begins to thicken. Don't overcook, or it will jell. Pour into sterilized jars and seal.

PICKLED HERRING

This is an original recipe of Ruth Bakke's. The idea of adding apple is Finnish, however. Norwegians don't put apples in.

2 cups sugar
1 cup water
4 cups vinegar
2 tablespoons pickling spice
6 or more salt herring
2 sliced onions
2 cups chopped apple

Boil together the sugar, water, vinegar, and pickling spice. Cool liquid and add salt herring which has been soaked overnight to remove salt. Add sliced onions. Before serving, add 2 cups of chopped apples.

CRISPY GARLIC DILL PICKLES

When the cucumbers ripen, head directly from the U-pick fields to your kitchen.

2 cups pickling salt
2 quarts cider vinegar
6 quarts water
Approximately 50 4-inch cucumbers
10-12 garlic cloves
10-12 heads of fresh dill

Wash and scrub cucumbers.

Combine pickling salt, vinegar, and water in large saucepan. Bring to a boil, then reduce to a simmer.

Pack cucumbers into hot, sterile quart jars. Add 1 clove of garlic and 1 head of fresh dill to each jar. Fill jars to within 1/2 inch of the top with hot brine.

Wipe jar rims well, apply lids, and process in boiling water bath for 20 minutes.

10 quarts

INDEX